Certification Manual

LEAN SIX SIGMA WHITE BELT

Collection: GESTIONA
Publishing director: David Soler

LEAN SIX SIGMA WHITE BELT. CERTIFICATION MANUAL
1st Edition, 2021

© 2021, Luis Vicente Socconini Pérez Gómez
© of this Edition: ICG Marge, SL

Publisher: Marge Books
València, 558 – 08026 Barcelona
Tel. 931 429 486 – marge@margebooks.com
www.margebooks.com

Edition coordination: Karina Ahumada Serrano
Edition: Mercedes Lara
Printed by: Safekat, SL (Madrid)

Paper Edition ISBN: 978-84-18532-99-3
Digital Edition ISBN: 978-84-19109-00-2
Legal Deposit:

The paper used in this books has not been bleached with elemental chlorine (CI_2).

The author

ABOUT LUIS SOCCONINI

He holds a bachelor's degree in Industrial Engineering and a master's degree in Quality and Productivity from Monterrey Tec. He is also a Master Black Belt in Lean Six Sigma and a distinguished professor at several prestigious universities in Mexico.

Luis is certified in Strategic Management by Stanford University, in Leading Product Innovation by Harvard University, and in Industry 4.0 by MIT.

He has worked as a business consultant for the Wharton Business School in Pennsylvania, as a process engineer for Grolsch Brewery in the Netherlands, and as a manufacturing engineer at IBM.

As director of Lean Six Sigma Institute, Luis develops high-impact projects for companies such as Abbott Laboratories, Kraft Heinz, Coca-Cola, BMW, Bimbo, and Fender – to name a few. He has a broad base of experience and is continually developing productivity applications in diverse industries such as construction, mining, agriculture, government, energy, service, and more.

Luis is the author of **Lean Six Sigma Green Belt, Certification Manual, Lean Company, Lean Manufacturing, The Process of the 5's in Action,** as well as co-author of **Lean Six Sigma Management System** and **Lean Energy 4.0.**

SOCCONINI

www.socconini.com

Index

Preface

Dear Reader,

I warmly welcome you on this journey to obtain the **Lean Six Sigma White Belt Certification** and I wish to congratulate you because having this certification manual in your hands means that you seek to contribute to social development through the improvement of people, processes, and organizations – which ultimately leads to the well-being of our communities.

This certification manual is born from the need to share what we at Lean Six Sigma Institute (LSSI) teach people who participate in organizational processes – including managers, business owners, government officials, engineers, operators, and students. All of them receive training to transform today's key processes and design the organizations of the future.

At first, this manual was part of the material delivered to LSSI course participants across the world. Until one day, our regional Director in Spain suggested that our manuals could also be distributed in bookstores – allowing anyone to access the knowledge that is revolutionizing business thinking and the way organizations work today. We know that as long as people are trained and – above all – committed to a new spectrum of design and improvement possibilities, organizations will grow stronger as they face the new challenges posed by the ever-changing world we live in.

In this manual you will find a particularly useful toolbox that will help you successfully develop and continuously improve organizational activities. This toolbox is the result of decades of best practices proven to help organizations maximize value and achieve their goals.

You will also find fundamental basic tools that every member of any organization must put into practice in order to establish a continuous improvement culture and system.

The work philosophy, tools, and methodologies explained in this manual will allow you to easily understand how the organizations of the future should be run – and will therefore enable you to become an agent of change and to produce positive, impactful results.

The goal of this certification manual is to help you understand and implement simple yet practical tools that you can also teach your colleagues and use to develop new ways of working – thus continuously adapting to complex, changing business environments.

In this world, improvement is optional – but progress is up to you. I appreciate your trust and confidence in giving us the opportunity to provide you with high-quality, widely tested material and I thank you for granting us the responsibility to guide you on this continuous improvement journey that starts but never finishes.

LUIS SOCCONINI
Founder and Director of Lean Six Sigma Institute

LEAN SIX SIGMA
WHITE BELT

Introduction to White Belt

Learning objectives

1. Understand the basic concepts and principles of Lean Six Sigma.
2. Understand the responsibilities associated with White Belts.
3. Learn how teamwork affects the Lean Six Sigma philosophy.
4. Understand Time Management techniques.

Content

> Background
> White Belt responsibilities
> Limitations to productivity
> Teamwork
> Time management

Evolution

Total Quality Control
Quality Circle
Just in time (JIT)
Supplier Development
Total Productive Maintenance (TPM)
Theory of Constraints (TOC)
Six Sigma
All Processes
Automation, Human Approach, and Sustainability
TQM
World Class
Lean Six Sigma Operation System
Lean Six Sigma Company
Lean Six Sigma 4.0
40s
50s
60s
70s
80s
90s
2010s
2020s

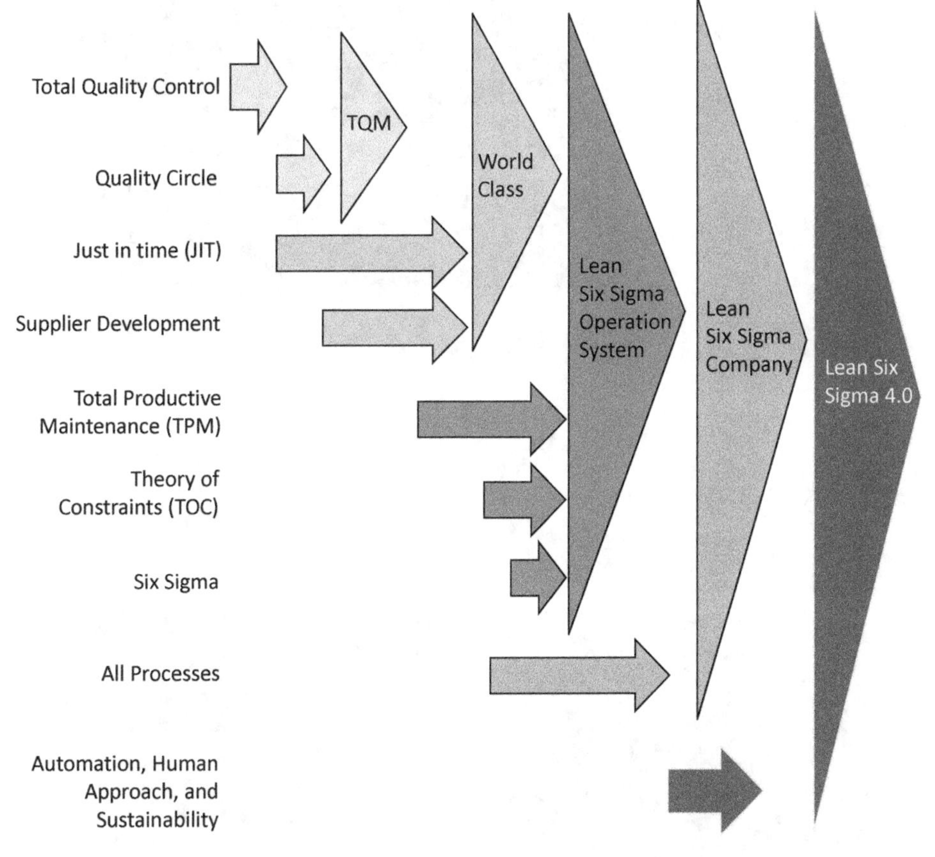

Time dedication

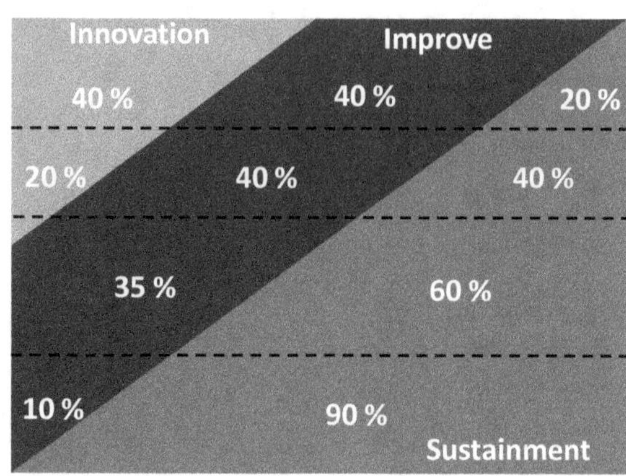

Lean Six Sigma tools

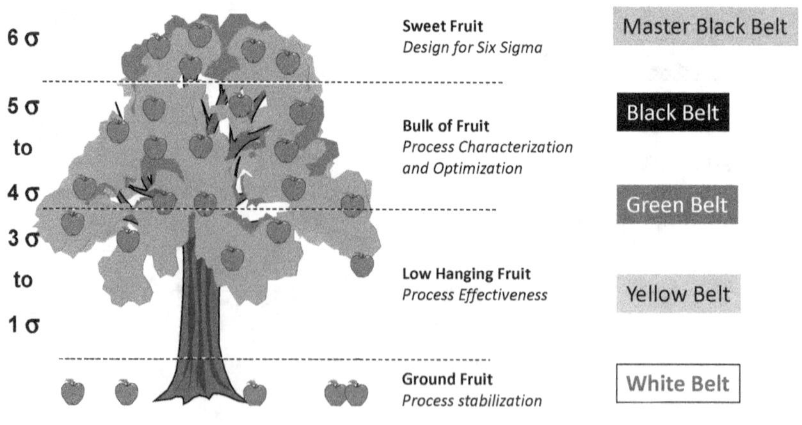

LSSI
LEAN SIX SIGMA INSTITUTE

White Belts responsibilities

Personally
- Keep their area clean and tidy.
- Manage their time correctly.
- Work with quality and on time.

Teamwork
- Identifies opportunities for continuous improvement.
- Participates in solving simple problems.
- Participates in improvement projects frequently.

Knowledge
- Lean Six Sigma Philosophy.
- Essential Tools.

Limitations to productivity

無理

無

駄

1. *Muri* = Overburden

2. *Mura* = Variability

3. *Muda* = Waste

Types of waste = Muda

Over-Production

Waiting & Searching

Pollution

Over-Processing

Transportation

Defects & Re-work

Unnecessary Movements

Excess Inventory

Energy

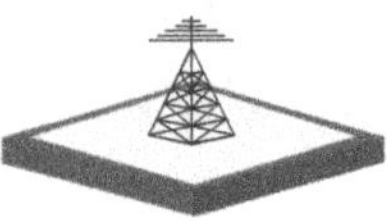

Non-Utilized Talent

Excess inventory = waste

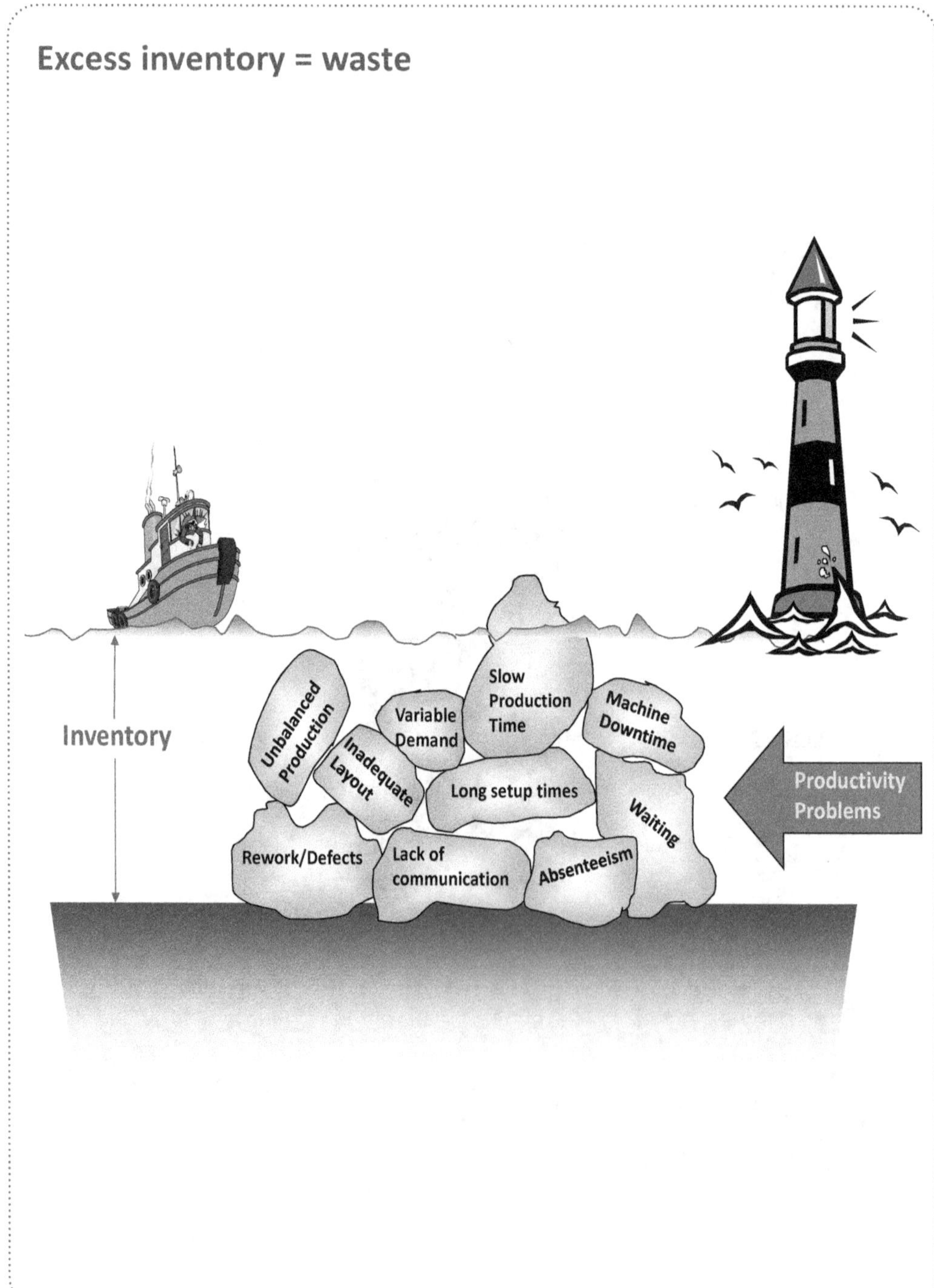

Traditional vs. Lean Model

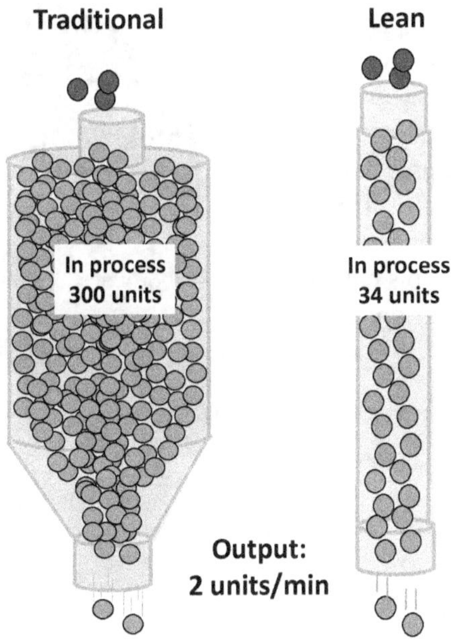

Find the difference in:

- Inventory cost (if $10/unit)
- Delivery speed
- Changeover time
- Space required

What is a team?

- A team is a group of people who perform interdependent tasks to work toward a common mission.

- **White Belts** are individuals that participate in teams and contribute ideas and actions to solve many problems with simple tools based on their individual job experience.

Types of teams

- **Process improvement teams** are project teams that focus on improving or developing specific business processes.

- **Work groups**, sometimes called "natural teams", have responsibility for a particular process (e.g., a department, a product line or a stage of a business process) and work together in a participative environment.

- **Self-managed teams** directly manage the day-to-day operation of their particular process or department.

White Belts **participate in every type of team and understand the team dynamics and the tools in order to maximize the results.**

Stages of team development

Forming > Storming > Norming > Performing

Forming

- Lack of integration or group maturity
- Effort to be pleasant among team members (complacent)
- Little progress in terms of work completed
- Roles and responsibilities are clarified and understood
- "Honeymoon" phase

Storming

- Team members start to voice their opinions
- The understanding of roles and responsibilities is questioned
- Conflict arises due to different ideas and conclusions
- Lack of agreement delays the team's work

Norming

- Team members resolve their conflicts
- The team reaches an understanding through mutually accepted ideas
- Some work is completed (team progress)
- Team members start to work as a team
- Trust is developed and more ideas are shared

Performing

- Synergy is created
- Interdependence is evident and accepted
- Team-based problem solving skills are developed
- Agreements are achieved
- Significant and noticeable progress in terms of work completed

Adapted from Bruce W. Tuckman.

Time management

- One of the most important causes of low team performance is a **lack of time management skills.**

- Time is one of the **most valuable resources.**

- By analyzing how we use our time, we will realize how we are wasting it and how we can find better ways to use it.

Parkinson's Law

It was first articulated by Cyril Parkinson in 1957 as a result of his research in the British Civil Service.

Examples:

- **Time**: work expands so as to fill the time available for its completion.
- **Income**: expenditures rise to meet income.
- **Space**: storage resources tend to increase (racks, drawers, etc.) to meet storage capacity.

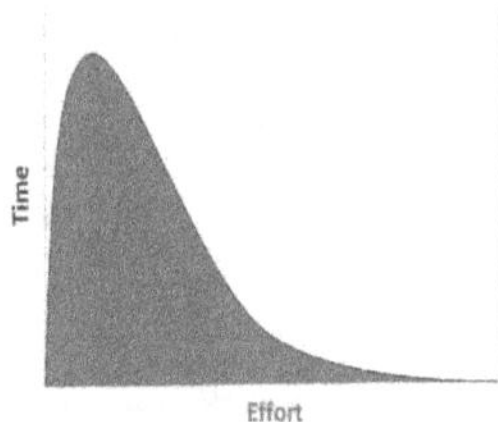

For many people, the more time they have to complete a task, the more their minds will wander, which can create problems.

LSSI
LEAN SIX SIGMA INSTITUTE

Time management best practices

1. Plan your day.

2. Use the Pomodoro Technique.

3. Use your email effectively.

4. Conduct effective meetings.

5. Make effective phone calls.

1. Plan your day

- Spend at least 15 minutes to plan your day.

- Schedule the activities in the medium to long-term.

- Plan daily life activities (exercise, food, transportation).

- Classify activities as A, B or C.

    - A: Important and urgent

    - B: Important and not urgent

    - C: Less important and not urgent

- When taking notes, define your tasks and schedule.

- Before you start your day, picture what your day will look like.

Daily planning example

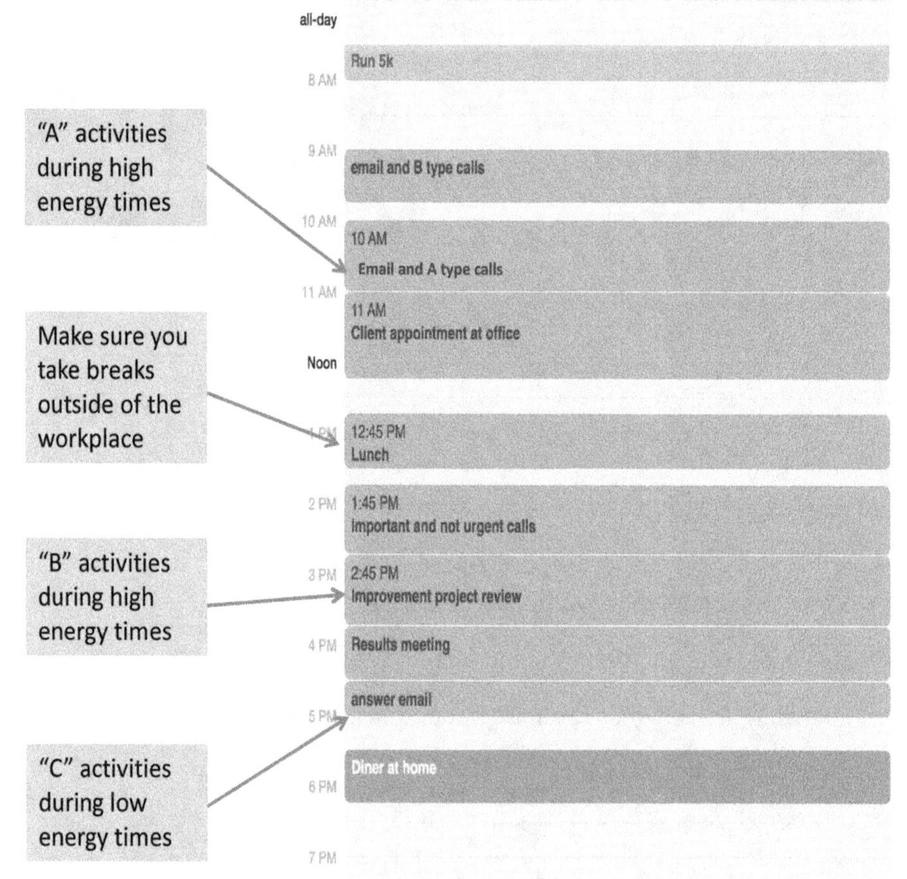

2. Use the Pomodoro technique

- The **Pomodoro Technique** is a time management method developed by Francesco Cirillo in the late 1980s.

- The technique uses a clock to divide the time spent on a job in 25-minute intervals - called "Pomodoros" - and separates them into short pauses.

A key objective of the technique is to eliminate (internal and external) interruptions.

1. Pick the task.
2. Set the Pomodoro (watch or clock) to 25 minutes.
3. Work on the task until the clock rings and record it with an X.
4. Take a short break (5 minutes).
5. After 4 "Pomodoro", take a longer break (15-20 minutes).

3. Use your email effectively

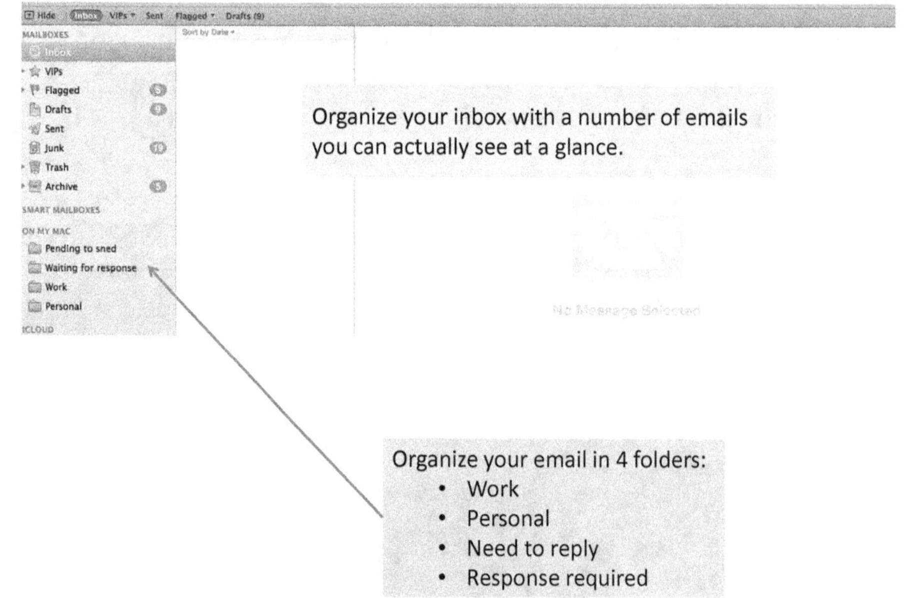

1. Answer only the emails you can complete in 2 minutes or less.
2. Eliminate the emails you don't need.
3. Archive the emails you need to keep.
4. Flag the emails you still need to reply to.

4. Conduct effective meetings

1. Plan the meeting
2. Send invitations
3. Confirm the logistics
4. Use an attendance sheet
5. Explain the objective of the meeting
6. Assign specific times during the meeting and follow them
7. Take notes
8. Write down the tasks to be completed and the person responsible
9. Summarize the meeting (confirm the objective)
10. Send a "meeting report" to all participants
11. Follow-up on the activities
12. Evaluate the meeting

Effective Meetings

Meeting #:

Date: Start time: End time: Actual Start Time: Act. End Time:

Type of Meeting:

Title:
Objective:
Location:

Leader:
Secretary:
Meeting Cost:

Participants

Name	Role	Attended?

Notes:

Agenda

Sequence	Topic	Time Alloted	Actual Time

Agreements

Agreements/Commitments	Person Responsible	Due Date	Notes

5. Make effective phone calls

1. Prepare for the conversation as if it was a meeting.

2. Group phone calls together so that you can continue with other calls if one number is busy.

3. Prioritize your calls.

4. Use the speakerphone or headset so you can continue with other activities (only type C calls).

5. Schedule your phone calls.

The ABCs for teamwork

- **A**chievement

- **B**elonging

- **C**ontribution

Problem Solving

2

Learning objectives

1. Apply a practical and simple method for defining problems.
2. Use a structured approach to understand the root cause of a problem.
3. Solve problems using a practical and simple methodology.

Content

> Background
> What is problem solving?
> Benefits
> When do we use the problem solving methodology?
> Methodology and example

Background

- Everyone faces different types of problems at work and personally.

- When trying to solve problems, most of the time we attack **symptoms** and **NOT causes**.

- How many of us know and apply a problem-solving methodology?

How do we normally solve problems?

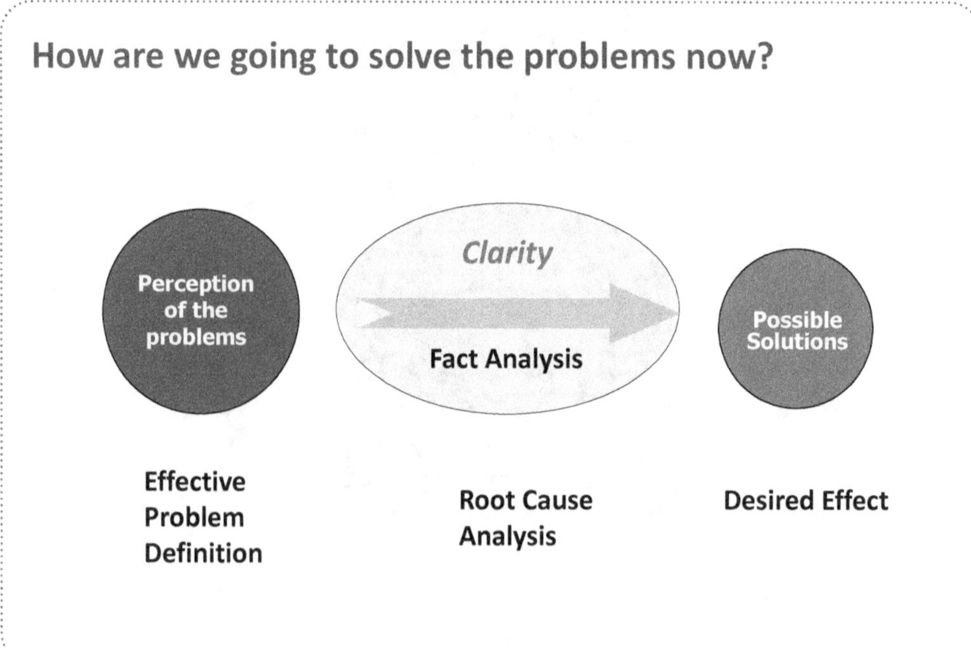

How are we going to solve the problems now?

Problem Solving

A methodology to solve problems based on the root cause.

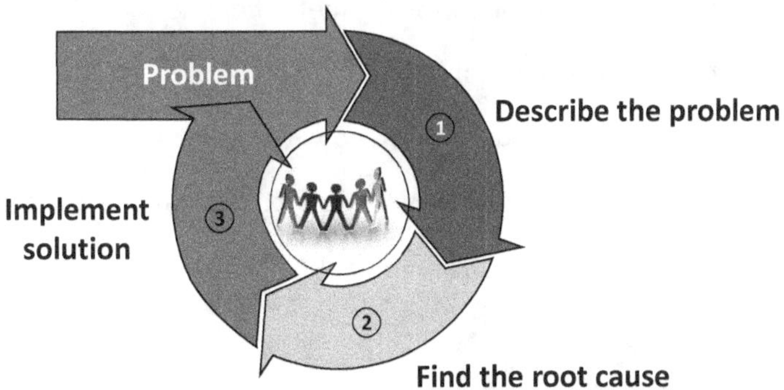

- It provides the team with an approach to define causes of the problem

- Prevents recurrence

- Create better standards

- Motivate teamwork

- It helps solve the problems permanently

«Working as a team ensures success.» Henry Ford

When do we use the problem solving methodology?

- The problem has been defined and quantified.

- The gap between a desired state and the current state justifies the use of a problem solving methodology.

- The root cause is not know.

- The need to act decisively and with urgency to resolve a problem.

- During the adaptation cycles to further enhance process control.

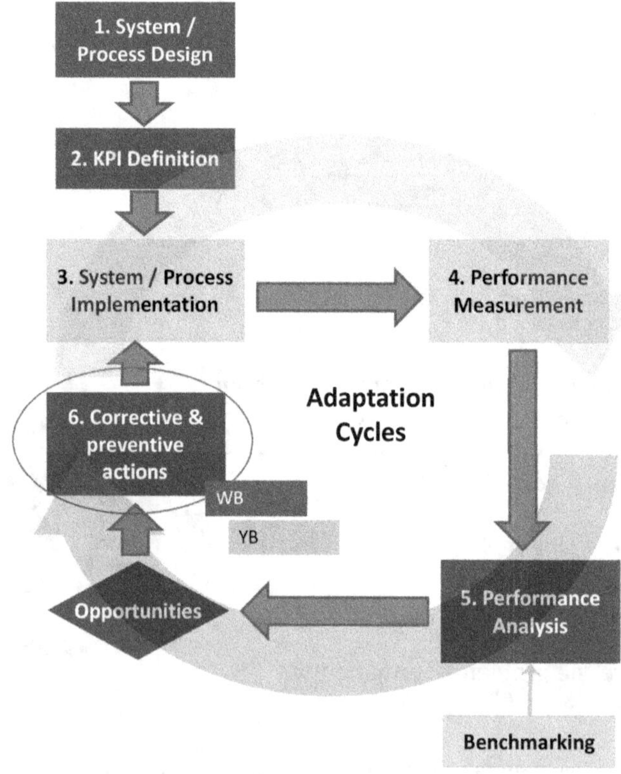

*KPI = Key Performance Indicator

How does it work?

Problem

STEP 1. DESCRIBE THE PROBLEM

Cause

STEP 2. FIND THE CAUSE

Solution

STEP 3. IMPLEMENT SOLUTION

PDCA - Share learning

1 **Problem**

- Define the problem as accurately as possible
- The problem is defined in the present tense

It should be written as a simple and concise statement that identifies the problem's subject using a present tense verb , along with the respective defect / situation.

Subject + present tense verb + (defect/situation)

Defect / situation is an undesirable characteristic, present in a product or process. **Subject** is the name given to a specific product or process containing the defect.

e.g. The pizza is delivered late.

Define the Problem

Find the Cause

Solution

The problem statement should comply with the following

1. **Be specific:** problems are usually stated vaguely:

   "The water is too hot."

2. **Describe the problem, not its symptoms:**

   "The morale of the department is low."

3. **Avoid causes and solutions:**

   "The response time for providing the service is the cause of the customer's dissatisfaction, which indicates a potential problem"

Use the brainstorming process to define the problem

- **Objective**: to express without bias all the opinions of the group.

- To achieve this goal, all participants should be asked to write on a small paper (post-its) all the ideas generated from the question:

  What do you think is the problem?

- The facilitator gathers and classifies all the ideas and presents them in an un-biased way.

SOS Example

Brainstorming

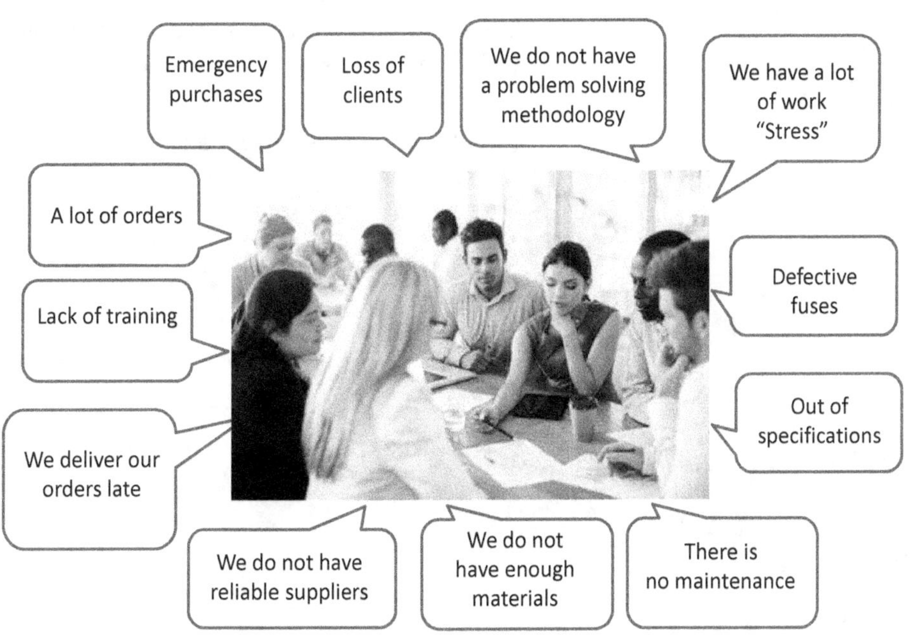

What is the problem?

2 Cause

Define the problem

Find the Cause

Solution

- Observe and answer **"Why does this happen?"**

- If you cannot answer the previous question: Use some of the basic tools for problem solving (fish diagram, 5 whys, current reality tree, etc.)

- Prioritize if there is more than one cause (use FACTS)

What is the cause?

Basic Tools

Fishbone Diagram (Ishikawa)

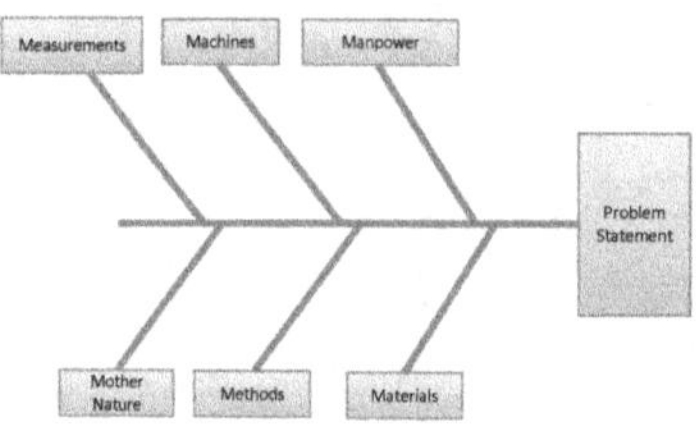

5 Whys

Current Reality Tree

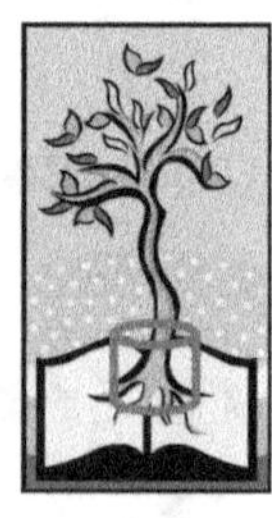

Fishbone Diagram / Ishikawa

Is a graphical tool that results from a brainstorming session in which all potential causes for a particular effect are listed and organized into categories. This makes it easier to separate problems and possible improvements.

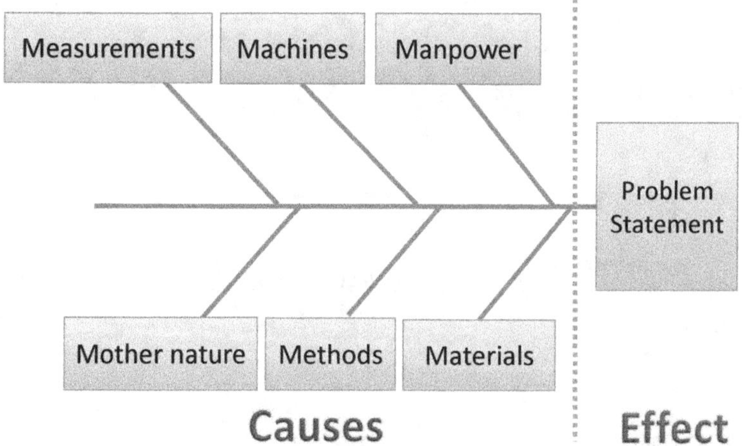

PROCEDURE

1. Define the problem.
2. Define categories.
3. Brainstorm in each category.
4. Verify ideas at the scene.
5. Mark the root causes in red.

Example S.O.S

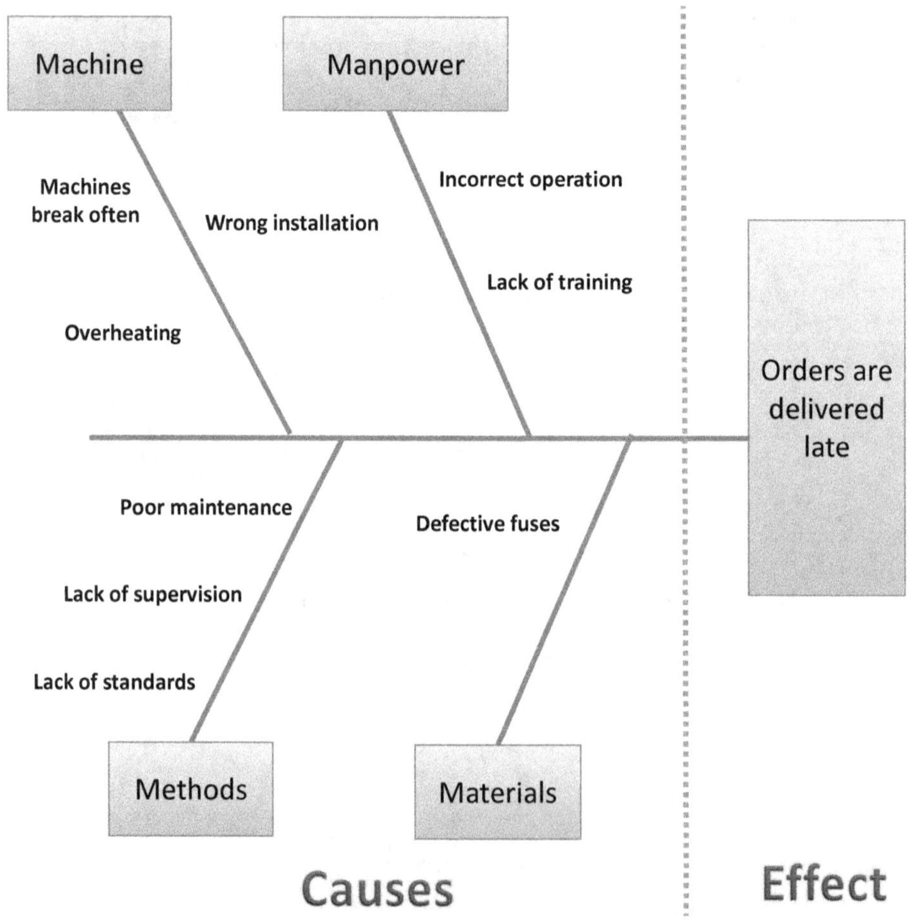
Machine
Manpower
Machines break often
Wrong installation
Incorrect operation
Lack of training
Overheating
Orders are delivered late
Poor maintenance
Defective fuses
Lack of supervision
Lack of standards
Methods
Materials
Causes
Effect

5 Whys

Define the problem:

Orders are delivered late to customers.

1. **Why?**
   - Because the machines are broken down

2. **Why?**
   - Because the fuses are melted

3. **Why?**
   - Because the machines are overheating

4. **Why?**
   - Because the oil changes are not made in time

5. **Why?**
   - Because there is no formal maintenance program

Current Reality Tree

A diagram that shows the **cause and effect relationships**, while taking into consideration all variables that influence a problem or a given situation. It includes circumstances, causes, effects, that pertain to the problem.

Eliyahu Goldratt

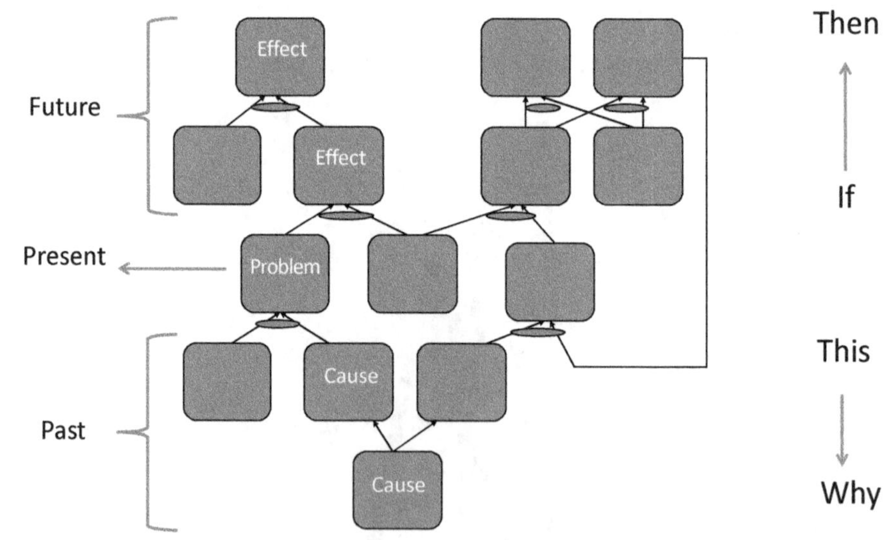

Example SOS

Develop a current reality tree

Find the cause (Solve)

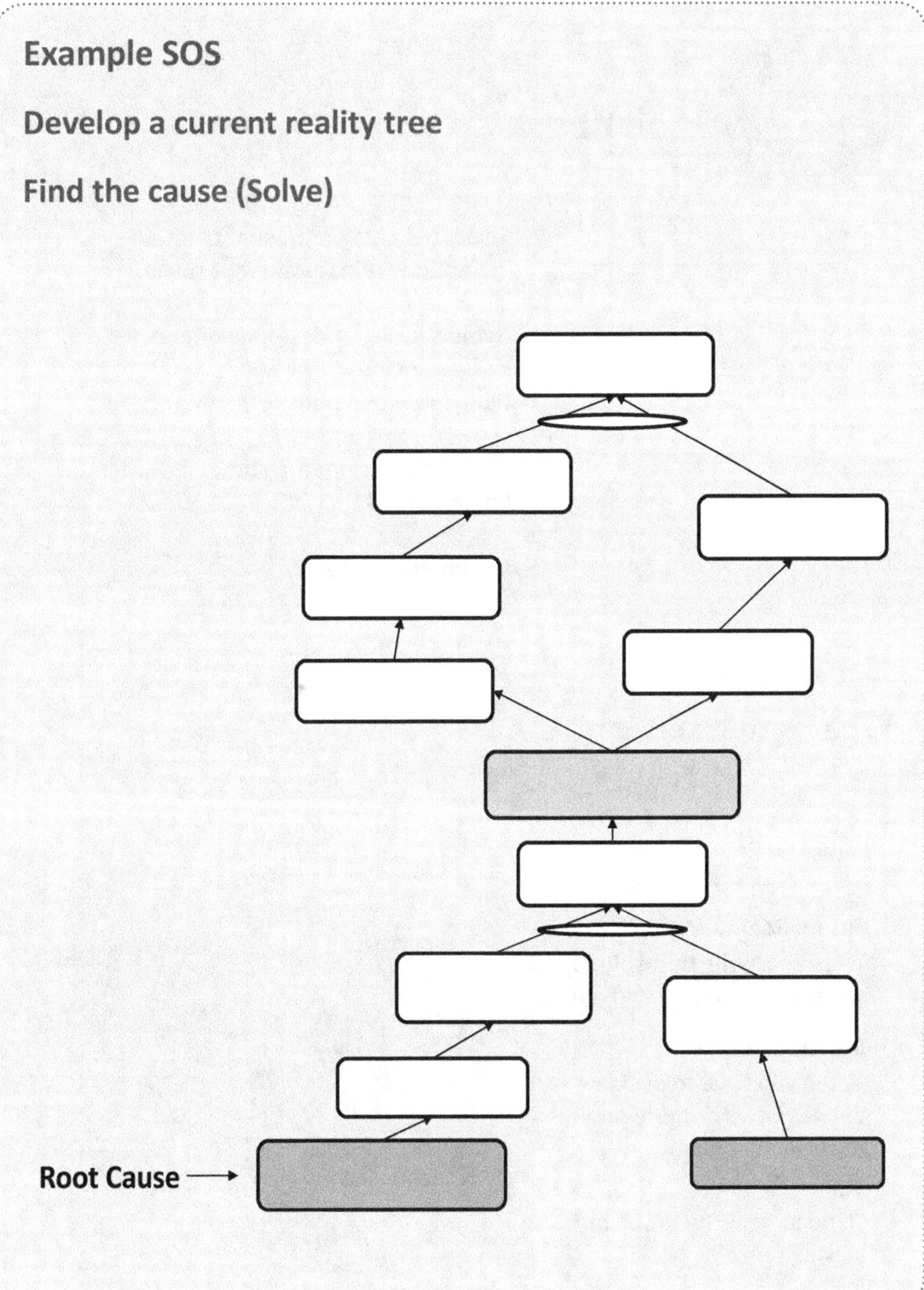

3 Solution

Define the problem

Find the cause

Solution

- Select the best permanent correct action to **eliminate the root cause**.

- **Avoid** causing **undesirable effects.**

- **Plan and implement** corrective actions.

- Verify that actions are **successful** when implemented.

- **Document** the case.

What is the solution?

Tools

- **Future Reality Tree**
  To establish the best solution sustained in actions and effects.

- **Decision Matrix**
  When you have to decide between two or more options to solve a problem.

- **A3**
  To document the problem solving process.

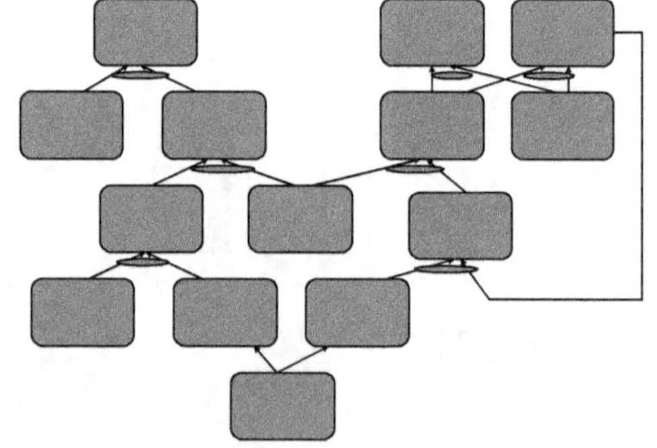

LSSI
LEAN SIX SIGMA INSTITUTE

Example SOS

Develop a Future Reality Tree

Solution (Solve)

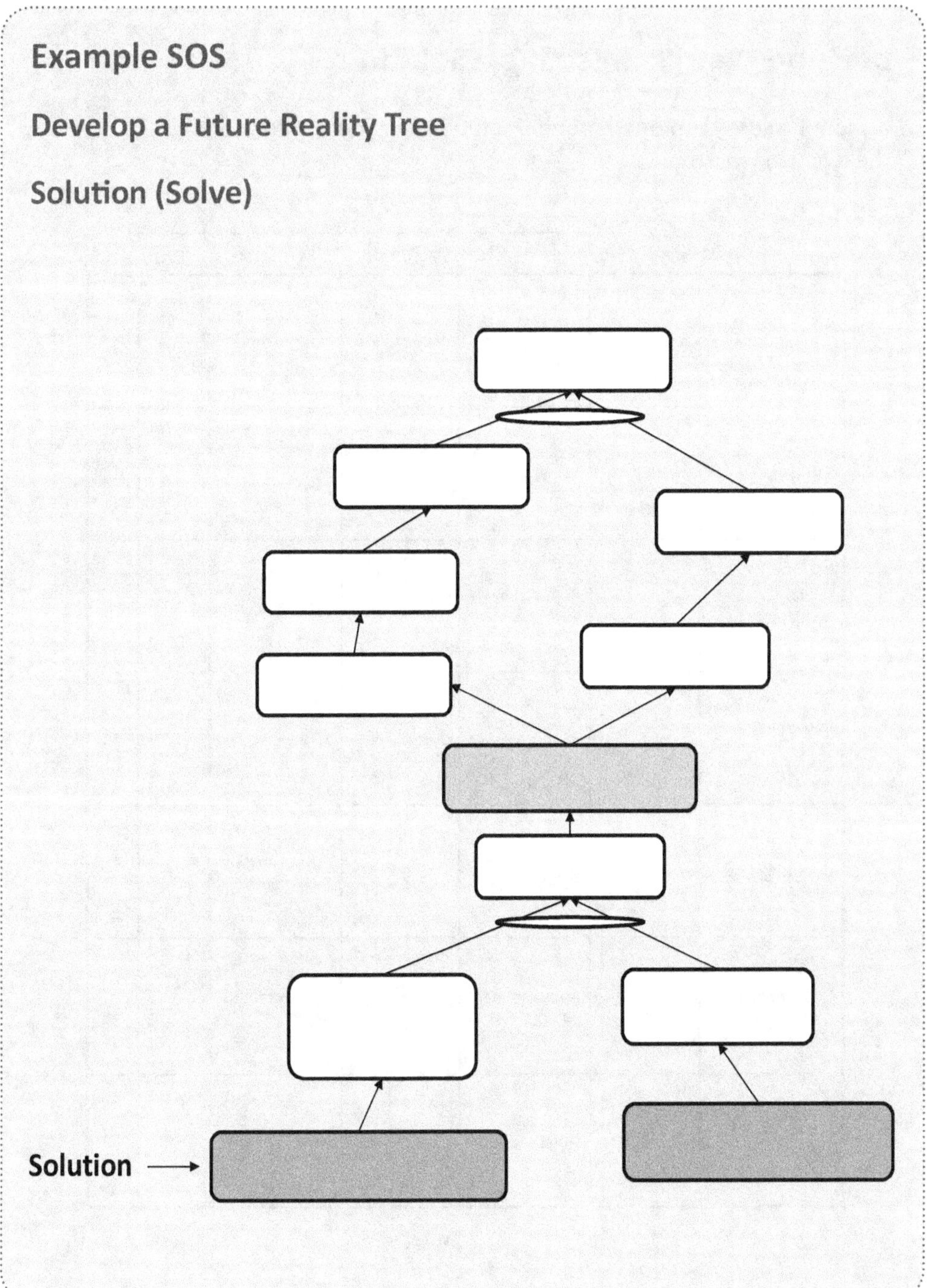

Decision Matrix: Selecting a Solution

If there is more than one potential solution to choose from, then use the following matrix:

Criteria	Importance	Alternative A			Alternative B		
		Evaluation	Value	Pts.	Evaluation	Value	Pts.
Safety	10	Visual fatigue	7	70	None	10	100
Defect Reduction	9	Reduced by 75%	8	72	Eliminated	10	90
Implementation Time	7	3 months	3	21	1 - 2 weeks	10	70
Operating Cost	5	Approximately $150/month	6	30	Approximately $25/month	9	45
Implementation Cost	3	Approximately $4,500	8	24	Approximately $5,000	6	18
Impact on Other Areas	2	None	10	20	None	10	20

Total 237 Total 343

Document the problem

Title: On time delivery, improving reliability

1. Background

Why are we talking about it?

- **Customers are complaining**
- **Late deliveries**
- **Low machine reliability**

2. Current Conditions

What's the problem, where do we stand?

- **Orders are not delivered on time**

3. Target/Goal(s)

What is the specific change you want to accomplish now?

- **Zero late deliveries**
- **Zero breakdowns**

4. Analysis

What is the root cause(s) of the problem?

- *Lack of preventive maintenance*
- *Operators don´t have the correct training*

Choose the simplest problem-solving tool for this issue:

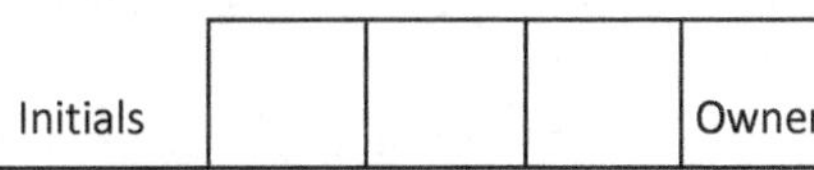

Initials | | | | Owner

Proposed Countermeasure(s)

Your proposal to reach the future state, the target condition.

- **Implement Total Productive Maintenance**
- *Develop a training program*

Plan

TPM Kaizen event	Days
	1 2 3 4 5
1 TPM Training	
2 Super cleaning event	
3 Generate opportunity cards	
4 Develop equipment FMEA	
5 Implement autonomous maintenance	
6 Develop prev. maint. calendar	
7 Develop prev. Maint. Instructions	
8 Implement visual controls	
9 Develop safety instructions	
10 Prepare operators and supervisors	

Performance indicators to track progress.

- **On-time delivery**
- **Overall Equipment Effectiveness**

Follow-up

- **Analyze box score in weekly meetings**
- *Gemba walks to analyze day by the hour boards*

What we accomplish?

- Apply the problem-solving process to:

    - Define the problem properly.
    - Identify the root cause and effects.
    - Define actions that eliminate the problem.
    - Efficiently document the problem-solving process.

- Now it is very important to consider:

    - Use the simple problem-solving method.
    - Teach our classmates, students and family how to solve problems in an easy way.
    - Constantly improve our problem-solving process.

Example SOS

Bayside is one of our best customers. Lately, we haven't been able to deliver a single order to them on time. Our facility is a mess. Nothing is ever produced as planned.

The production supervisor blames maintenance personnel for being too slow when fixing maintenance issues. The maintenance staff blames the operators for not taking care of the machines and letting them breakdown constantly. The bottom line is that we are not delivering products on time to our customers, and they are assessing the possibility of going with other more reliable suppliers.

Every day, we try our best to meet our production schedule. However, issues keep coming up, and as the production manager, I spend much of my time resolving them.

In the last few days, we have had to pay for excessive maintenance costs and overtime to ensure that our orders are complete. However, we still can't meet our expected delivery dates and requirements.

I really don't know what is going on with the company. I am beginning to feel desperate and am not sure what the solution is. I have morning meetings every day with my production personnel and we review the production schedule. The meetings are chaotic since everyone is placing blame on each other and no one can agree on the best problem solving method.

In the maintenance report, I have noted high reliability/performance fuses are being changed frequently. Lately, I have had to approve urgent purchase orders for fuses to avoid stopping the production machines.

I think we need to establish a preventive maintenance plan, but with all the problems we are facing, I don't see how we can put one together since there is not enough time to focus on both production and maintenance.

The operators are constantly reporting that the machines are overheating, but I think they are just using the machines as an excuse to evade their responsibility for not meeting production and delivery requirements. I have been wanting to launch a training program to teach the operators how to operate the machines correctly, but we haven't had time since we are almost always behind schedule.

At this point, I don't know what the solutions are to address our problems and I am totally overwhelmed. I need to solve our issues quickly or we might have to completely shut the plant down due to low productivity.

5S Housekeeping

3

Learning objectives

1. Understand the benefits of working in a clean and orderly environment.
2. Learn how to implement the 5S discipline

Content

> Background
> What is 5S Housekeeping?
> Benefits
> Procedure
> Examples

Why is order important?

I cannot find my keys!

Where did I put that document?

Where are those materials?

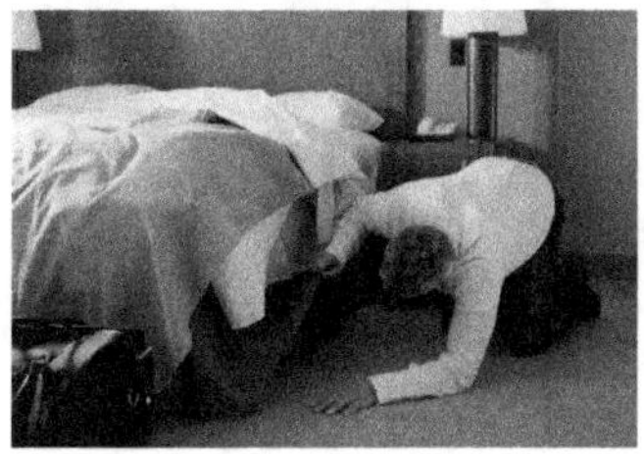

Hiroyuki Hirano

- Culture and habits are the most important elements of agile thinking (Lean Thinking).

- 5S was developed by Hiroyuki Hirano and is considered a stepping stone to other improvement tools or systems.

- Therefore, it is said that a good improvement event is one that starts with 5S.

Origin of the 5Ss   1950

- Ford Motor Company developed the CANDO program.
- The Japanese, who visited the Ford Michigan plants, adopted it (Hiroyuki Hirano).

C leaning up   *= Seiri*

A rranging   *= Seiton*

N eatness   *= Seiso*

D iscipline   *= Seiketsu*

O ngoing Improvement = Shitsuke

Toyota improved Ford's design

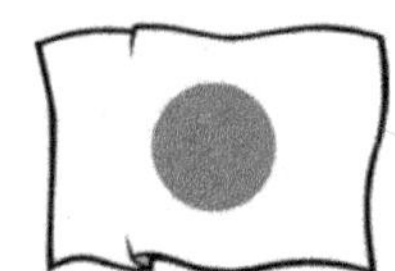

LSSI
LEAN SIX SIGMA INSTITUTE

What is 5S Housekeeping?

- 5S is a **discipline** that improves productivity in the workplace by standardizing **housekeeping habits** (orderliness and cleanliness).

What is NOT 5S Housekeeping?

- A methodology that is only applicable to manufacturing environments.
- A program to impress visitors and customers.
- A spring cleaning event.
- A system that has little impact on efficiency and customer satisfaction.

Benefits

- Find anything in less than 30 seconds
- Improved employee productivity
- Improved personal satisfaction
- Safer work environment
- Higher Quality

A **5S program** is well-developed with the successful completion of the following steps:

Sort	Straighten	Shine	Standardize	Sustain
Separate the necessary items from the unnecessary items.	Organize the necessary work items by establishing a specific place for each item.	Clean the workspace and keep it neat.	Define methods to ensure that the procedures and activities are implemented consistently.	Make a habit out of 5S activities to ensure that work areas are more productive.

Sort – Seiri

Sort > Straighten > Shine > Standardize > Sustain

Sort: Remove all the items from the workplace that are not necessary for performing productive operations.

Sorting process:

1. Recognize areas of opportunity

2. Define the selection criteria

3. Identify the selected items

4. Make the selected items available

1. Recognize areas of opportunity

- Warehouses
- Common areas
- Offices
- Production floor
- Briefcases
- Binders
- Computers

2. Define the selection criteria

You must decide what to do with the items that are **not needed.**

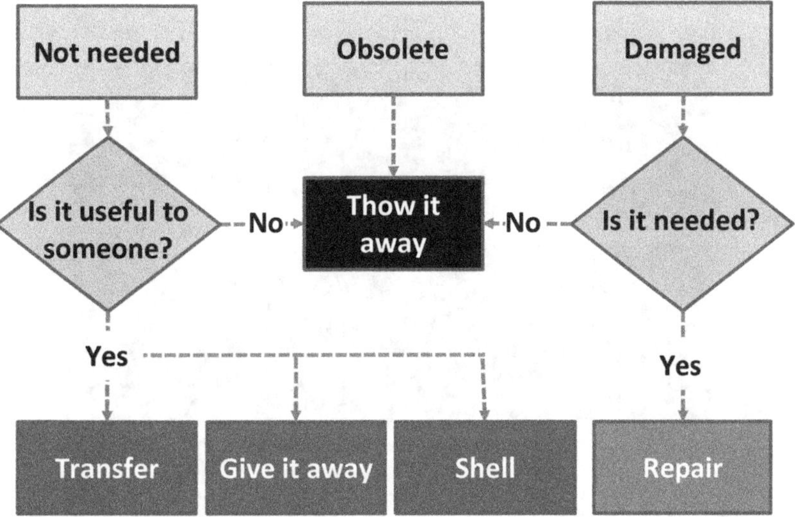

- Select what is not needed.

- Go through all work areas, shelves, drawers, etc. Keep only essential items. Store or discard everything else.

3. Identify the selected items

The items categorized as **not needed** must be clearly labeled and confined in a quarantine area.

Seiri **Principle**

«Only what is needed, only the amount needed and only when you need it.»

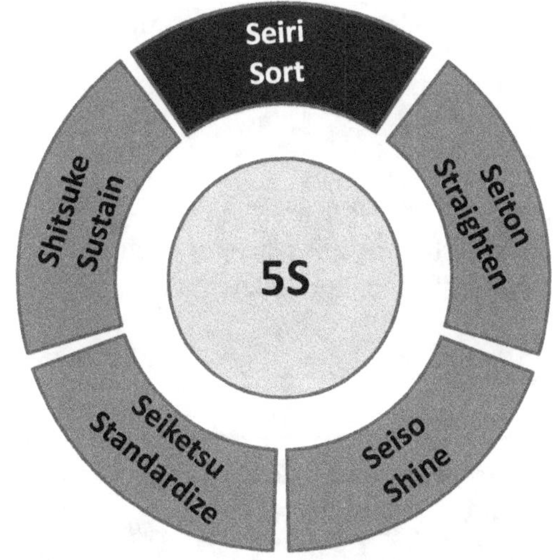

Straighten – Seiton

Sort > **Straighten** > Shine > Standardize > Sustain

Straighten: Organize necessary work items and establish a specific place for each item. This will facilitate item identification, location, availability, and return after use.

Straightening process:
1. Prepare the work area
2. Establish a specific place for each item
3. Establish rules and follow them

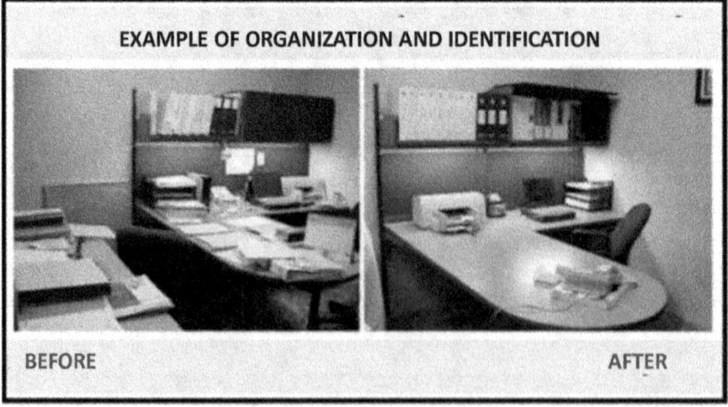

LSSI
LEAN SIX SIGMA INSTITUTE

Key elements

- All needed items have a designated location.
- The need to search for items is eliminated.

Value

- Everything is organized and accessible.
- There is a place for everything.
- After use, items are returned to where they belong.

- Determine how long it takes to find the items.

  - **Can you find any item in less than 30 seconds?**

- When organizing, focus on:

  - Defining the location for the parts, tools, supplies, and materials based on their function.

  - Clearly identifying the items' names and locations.

  - The ability to quickly and easily retrieve the items.

- **Deliverable:**

  - A list of necessary items, where they can be found, and locations that are clearly marked.

1. Prepare the work area

Color Codes for 5S

	Physical Health Hazard Exposure area
	Fire & Emergency Equipment
	Operational Clearance Area
	Permanent Location for Equipment
	Defects, Scraps, Rework, Red Tag area
	Working Areas & Aisleways
	Finished Goods, Completed Documentation/Paperwork
	Temporary Storage Location, Waiting for approval

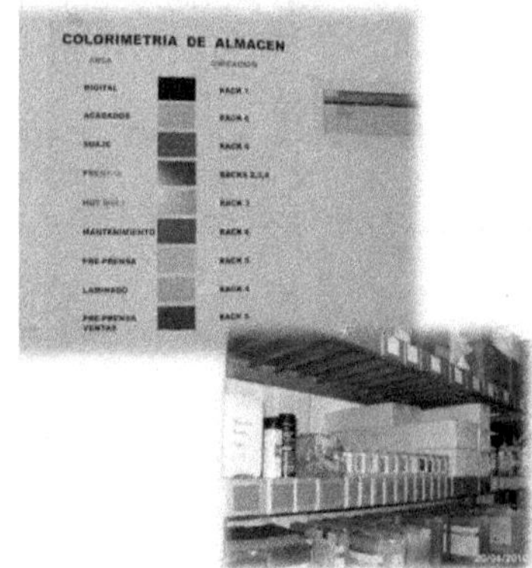

2. Establish a specific place for each item

"Anyone" can immediately see, retrieve and return any item.

Question	Answers
What?	Define which items are necessary (select)
	Identify the items
Where?	Define their correct location
	Mark their locations to make them identifiable
How many?	Define the quantity of items
	Identify the number of items needed

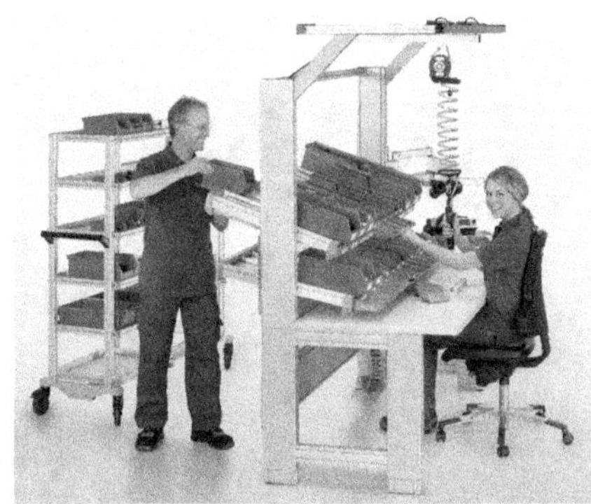

▶ What?

- Define which items are required

- Use removable labels to clearly identify an item and use another label to specify where it should be kept

Provide specific and accessible locations for each item

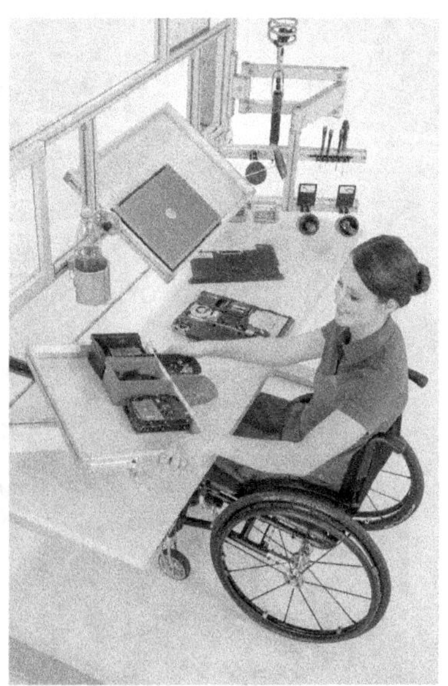

▶ Where?

Store all items that are used together in the same location.

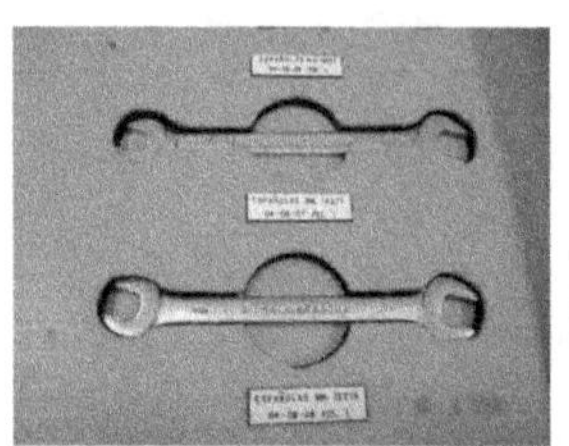

Store items with similar functions together.

Avoid storing items in enclosed spaces.

Each item is in its place

Cabinet Identification

- Use letters to identify cabinets

- Arrange the cabinets in rows and column

- Name files and folders

LSSI
LEAN SIX SIGMA INSTITUTE

▶ How many?

Seiton Principle

«A place for everything, and
everything in its place.»

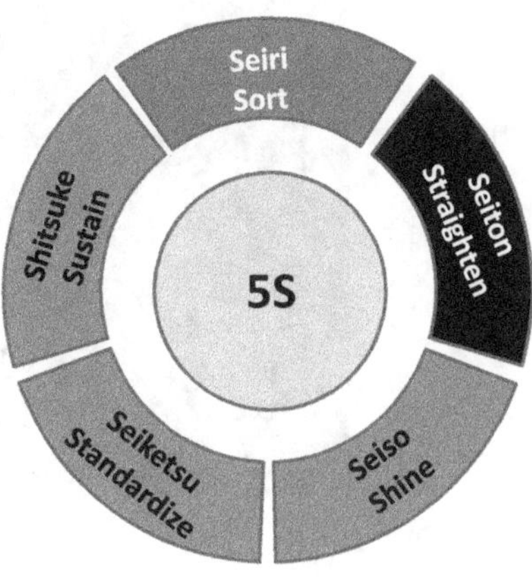

Shine – Seiso

Sort Straighten **Shine** Standardize Sustain

Shine: Very simple. Clean the workspace! Remove all the dirt.

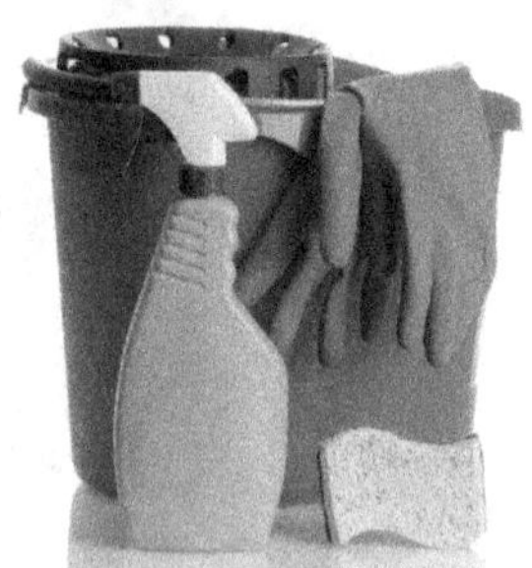

Cleaning process:

1. Create a cleaning schedule

2. Define cleaning methods

3. Develop discipline

Cleaning process

In Japan, children start the day cleaning their schools as a way of respecting and caring for the environment where they will learn the knowledge for life.

LSSI
LEAN SIX SIGMA INSTITUTE

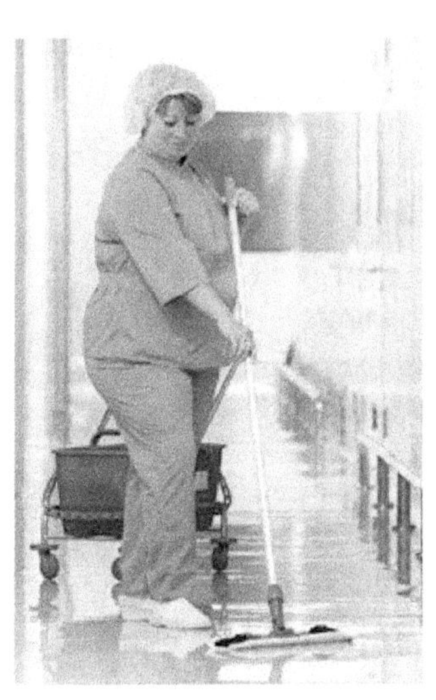

Shine – Useful tips

- Identify sources of dirt
- Always inspect while cleaning
- Repair leaks to prevent soiling
- Paint areas, equipment, floors, walls, and ceilings
- Improve lighting in the work areas

1. Create a cleaning schedule

Determine who is responsible for the cleaning activities, and define when and how often each activity should take place.

Cleaning Schedule				
Area	Items	Responsible	Shift	Frequency
Prens #1	Floors	J. Hobbs	1st	Daily
	Prenss	M. Hilton	2nd	Weekly
	Lamps	H. Patrick	3rd	Weekly
	Conveyor	J. Chase	2nd	Daily

2. Define cleaning methods

- Make a list of all cleaning activities
- Make a list of the items, supplies, and equipment needed
- Document the cleaning activities

▶ **Step approach to cleaning**

Common areas: surfaces, walls, ceilings, lights, storage areas, bathrooms, shelves, filing cabinets, etc.

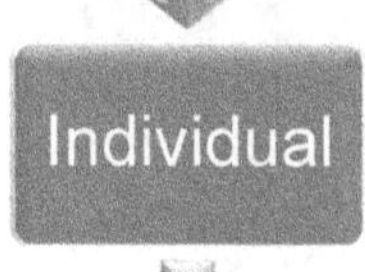

Individual work stations: chairs, drawers, computers, shelves, etc. Clean things under your table!

Measuring instruments: micrometers, calibrators, Vernier calipers, microscopes, etc.

Seiso **Principle**

«The cleanest place is not the one cleaned the most,
but the one that gets dirty the least.»

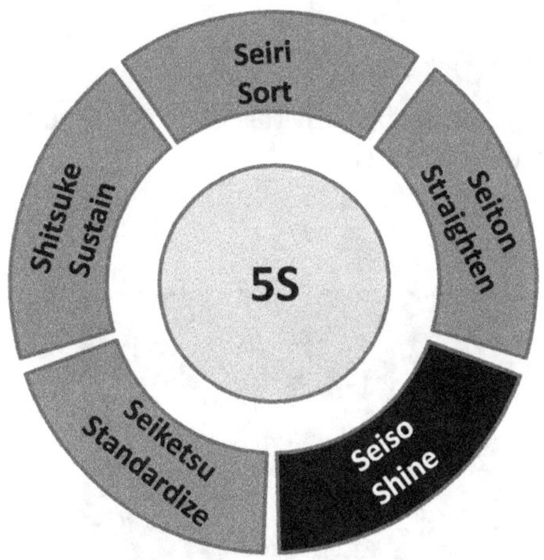

Standardize – Seiketsu

Sort Straighten Shine **Standardize** Sustain

Standaize: Ensure that procedures, practices, and activities are implemented consistently and on a regular basis. Ensure that the *Sort*, *Straighten* and *Shine* stages are maintained in the work areas

Standardize process:

1. Integrate the 5S activities into your regular work day
2. Evaluate the results

1. Integrate the 5S activities into your regular work day

- Establish procedures
- Develop a standardization manual
- Perform inspections

▶ Evaluate the areas

5S Audit			
AREA AUDITED	**AUDITING TEAM**	**SIGNATURES**	
DATE	**AUDITED TEAM**	**SIGNATURES**	

		AUDIT ITEMS	SCORE
SORT	1.1	There is a list of required items in the work area	
	1.2	The quantity of required items in the work area has been established	
	1.3	The required items are in good condition for use	
	1.4	The list of required items matches what is actually in the work area	
	1.5	The aisles and work areas are free of obstacles and unnecesary items	
	1.6	Unnecesary items were either sent to the quarantine area, thrown away, relocated or sold	
		Total	
STRAIGHTEN	2.1	Location codes have been established for each item in the list of required items	
	2.2	Locations have been established for each item (equipment, tools, materials, etc.)	
	2.3	Identification methods have been established and standardized (color coding, location codes, organization and labeling of racks and tools)	
	2.4	Areas have been taped off according to color codes	
	2.5	The locations and codes are respected for each item (the required items are properly identified and in their place)	
	2.6	There is visual information that communicates the organization of areas, objects and required items	
	2.7	The information which is posted is up to date	
	2.8	It is possible to identify when something is out of place	
	2.9	It is possible to find any item in 30 seconds or less	
		Total	
SHINE	3.1	Work areas are clean	
	3.2	Tools and required items are clean	
	3.3	Methods have been established to prevent areas/items from getting dirty	
	3.4	Cleaning schedules have been established and cleaning activities are documented	
	3.5	The required cleaning supplies and equipment is available and in good conditions	
	3.6	The team members' appearance looks clean (Uniform, shoes, face, etc.)	
		Total	
STANDARDIZE	4.1	Color coding, labels and written signs have been standardized	
	4.2	Furniture, tooling, work items, work materials, etc have been standardized	
	4.3	The use of safety equipment has been standardized (for those operations that require it)	
	4.4	A standardization manual has been established (5S rules, item locations, area layout, racks, etc.)	
	4.5	Completed last weeks' audit of the corresponding area in a timely manner	
		Total	

OBSERVATIONS	Scoring Guide
	0 = Implementation between 0 and 20%
	1 = Iimplementation between 20 and 40 %
	2 = Implementation between 40 and 60 %
	3 = Implementation between 60 and 80 %
	4 = Implementation between 80 and 90 %
	5 = Implementation between 90 and 100 %

LSSI
LEAN SIX SIGMA INSTITUTE

2. Evaluate the results

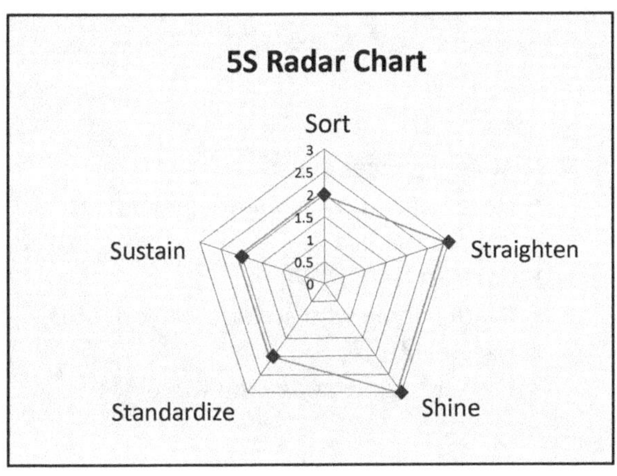

Seiketsu Principle

«Say what you do,

do what you say,

and prove it.»

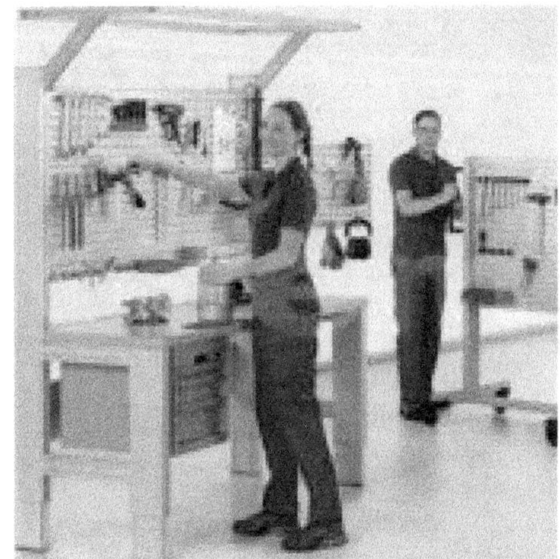

Sustain – Shitsuke

Sort > Straighten > Shine > Standardize > **Sustain**

Sustaining never ends:
- Have follow-up / monitoring meetings
- Improve standards
- Conduct Gemba Walks
- Invite people who are outside your area
- Have contests
- Publicly acknowledge the successes

Suggestions for implementation

Preparation
- Management training
- Train all staff
- Define the implementation team
- Define pilot area(s)
- Divide areas
- Create visual control boards
- Design a logo and theme
- Take pictures of the areas
- Kick-off day

Implement 1st S
- Apply first 5S evaluation
- Photos of current state
- Training on 1st S
- Red cards
- Sort and classify
- Verify red cards
- Evaluation (check list)
- Pictures of improvements

Implement 2nd S
- Progress review and training on 2nd S
- Start organizing and labeling
- Verify
- Evaluation (check list with pictures of 2nd S)
- Pictures for future evaluations

Implement 3rd S
- Progress review and training on 3rd S
- Establish cleaning schedules
- Verify
- Evaluation (check list with pictures of 2nd S
- Pictures of improvements

Implement 4th S
- Create standardization manual
- Create evaluation forms/templates
- Create order and cleanliness regulations

In the industry

Manufacturing plant

Warehouse

Workshops

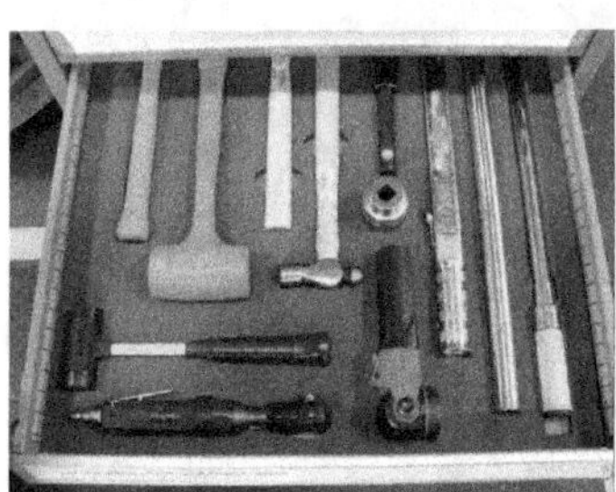

Workstation / Storage

All materials are identified and in their designated places.
Wheels are installed under the storage units for easy movement.

Laboratory

In documents and files

LSSI
LEAN SIX SIGMA INSTITUTE

In office

Visual Management (Andon)

Learning objectives

1. Understand how visual management works as an essential part of the Lean transformation.
2. Leverage visual tools to improve operational structure and stability, reduce variation, and increase efficiency.
3. Apply visual tools in your daily routines to improve efficiencies in both your work and personal life.

Content

> Background
> What is Andon?
> Benefits
> Procedure
> Examples
> Exercise

Background

Long ago, early humans painted on cave walls as a form of communication and establish a legacy.

Historically, armies recognized one another by their flags and uniforms.

How do humans perceive information?

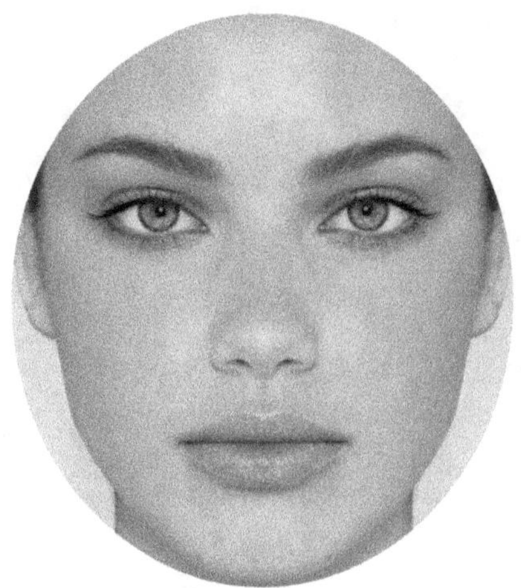

83 % by Sight

11 % by Hearing

4 %   by Smell

1 %   by Touch

1 %   by Taste

Origin of Andon

- In ancient Japan, an Andon was a **lamp**.

- It was made of sheets of paper placed around a base, with a candle inside.

- An Andon was used as a **visual signal** to communicate a message over long distance.

What is Andon?

- Andon is a signal that incorporates **visual, auditory, and textual elements,** and is used to notify people of quality issues or stoppages due to specific reasons.

- Information provided by these signals can be used to identify or indicate a **regular or irregular condition** at the workplace, which might require further action.

- Andon provides real-time information and feedback on the status of a process.

- These signals are efficient, self-regulating, and managed by the operators.

What is NO Andon?

- A presentation of screens and graphics to impress corporate visitors or customers
- An opportunity to fill up space on bare walls for decorative purposes
- A one-time effort, where visual elements or information become obsolete over time
- An isolated application of Leader Standard Work

Key Points

- Visual management is an essential part of a Lean management system.
- For visual management to be effective and sustainable, it must be integrated with:

  - Strategic management
  - Management follow-up (Gemba walks)
  - Situation analysis (Kata)
  - Standardized work
  - Project management
  - Daily management

  - Results management
  - 5S Housekeeping
  - Continuous flow
  - Quick preparations
  - Total Productive Maintenance
  - Kanban
  - Etc.

Which of the following ANDON elements can you identify in the photo?

- Materials
- Methods
- Machines
- Workforce
- Measurements
- Environment
- Safety

LSSI
LEAN SIX SIGMA INSTITUTE

Form of communication

- A distinctive aspect of visual communication is that it helps to guide the activities of group members, so that everyone is working in the same direction.
- **An Andon can be a:**
  - Signal
  - Sound
  - Label
  - Screen
  - Trend chart
  - Color scheme
  - Etc.

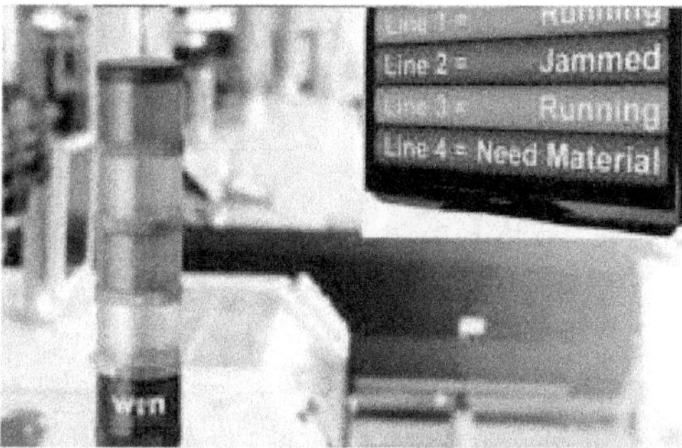

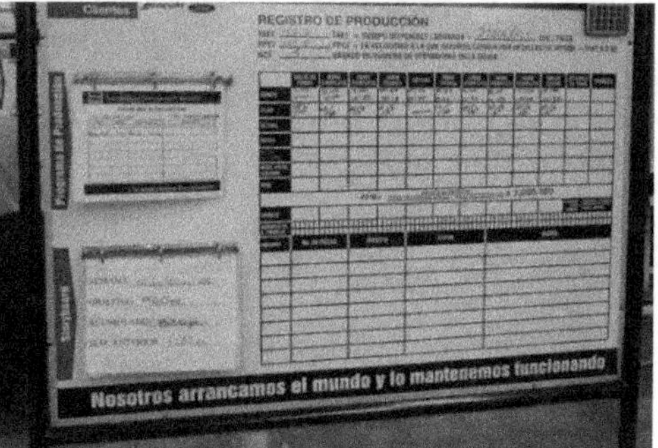

Andon example - Turning off car lights

Visual Control Levels combined with Poka-yoke

1. Share Information	Include instructions to "turn off the lights before turning off the engine" in the car's owner's manual.
2. Share established standards	Write the instructions on the car's dashboard so that it is easy for the driver to see them: "The lights should be turned off before leaving the car."
3. Incorporate standards in the workplace	Install a red light near the instructions so that both are easily seen by the driver.
4. Notification of irregular condition	Install a bell that sounds immediately when you open the car door if the lights are on.
5. Detection of irregular condition	Install a device that prevent the keys from being removed from the ignition if the lights are on.
6. Prevent irregular condition	Install a device that automatically turns off the lights when the engine is turned off.

Benefits

- Improves **Quality**
- Reduces **Costs**
- Improves **Response Time**
- Improves **Safety**
- Improves **Communication**

- Provides a way to bring **Immediate attention** to a problem
- Offers a **simple mechanism** to communicate information
- Improves **accountability**
- Increases the **speed and quality** of decision-making

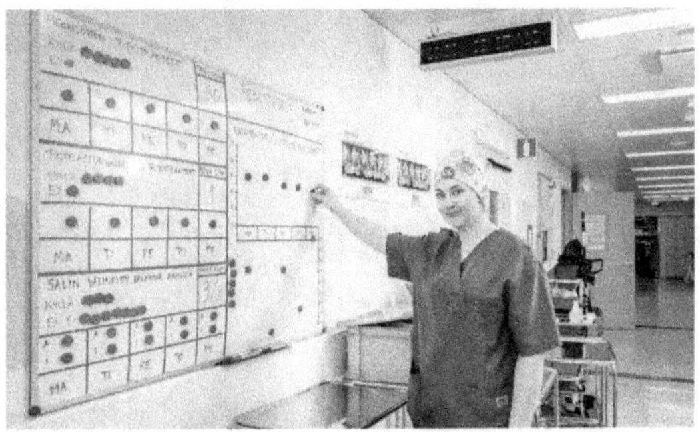

Procedure

1. Identify the information you want to know and the errors you want to avoid.

2. Design a simple visual way to guide and manage the activities of the group members.

3. Test the method – Seek feedback from the involved group members.

4. Train the entire group so that everyone is using the system.

5. Review and improve the system regularly.

Andon is widely applicable in both Services and Manufacturing.

Services and production

- Hospitals and clinics
- Restaurants
- Laboratories
- Manufacturing facilities
- Logistics operations
- etc.

Hospitals

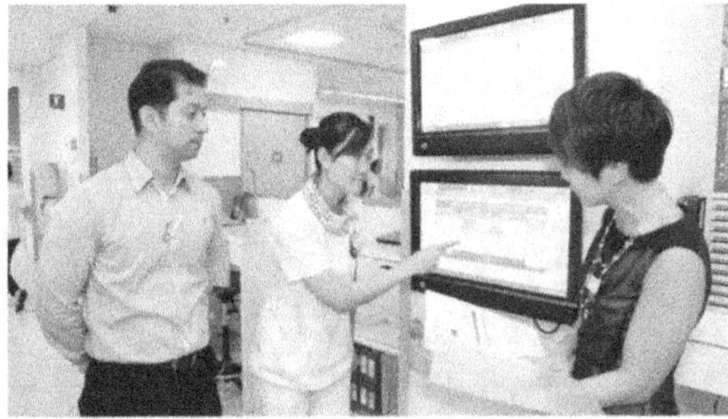

Hospital admissions

Dashboard

Agile meetings

- Andon Boards.
- Only relevant information is discussed.
- All participants are well-informed.
- All participants contribute ideas.
- A plan is suggested.
- Everyone shares common goals.

Source: Products Verde Valle.

Andon in manufacturing cells

Use Andon to compare the actual results against the goals every hour.

- Leaders and operators meet every day at the beginning of the shift.

- Goals and requirements are established.

- During the shift, the operators update the information every hour. Decisions are made based on the results.

MACHINE #23

HOUR	TARGET	ACTUAL	CUMMULATIVE TARGET	CUMMULATIVE ACTUAL	DEFECTS	COMMENTS
7:00 – 8:00	95	90	95	90	1	Morning meeting went over – material not secured during startup
8:00 – 9:00	100	100	195	190	0	
9:00 – 10:00	100	100	295	290	0	
10:00 – 11:00	100	100	395	390	0	
11:00 – 12:00	75	75	470	465	0	
12:00 – 1:00	75	40	545	505	0	Changeover
1:00 – 2:00	100	90	645	595	3	Changeover – Startup issues, incorrect program
2:00 – 3:00	100	100	745	695	0	
3:00 – 4:00	85	85	830	780	0	

Andon in Product Family / Value Stream

- The Value Stream team meets to analyze results.

- Both the current state and future state VSMs for the next 2-4 months are shown.

- The strategies, structure, and talent program are analyzed.

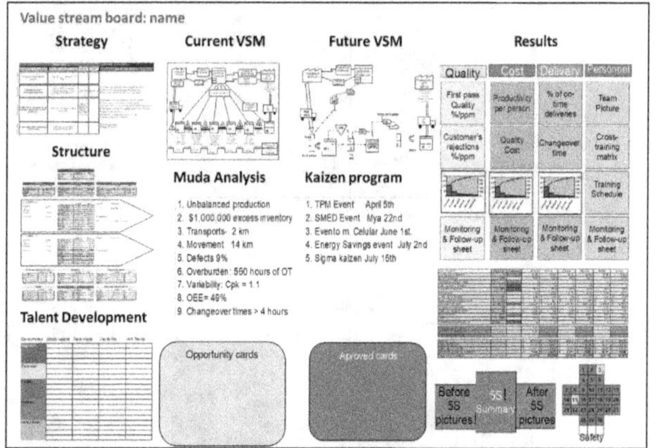

Tips for creating a visual space

- Mark all inventory areas.

- Mark the places where the equipment belongs with labels.

- Indicate visually the amount of paperwork allowed.

- Label all cabinets, shelves, etc., with their designated content.

Safety Andons

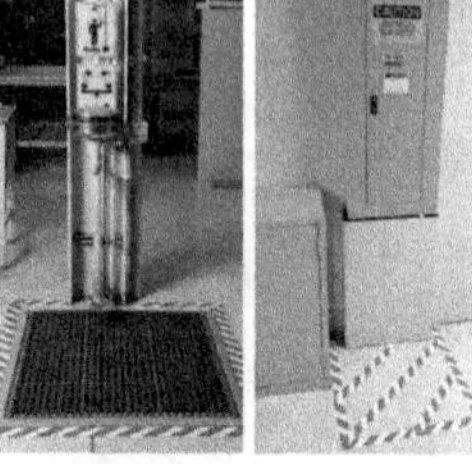

Hazardous materials

Area that required use of personal protective equipment (PPE)

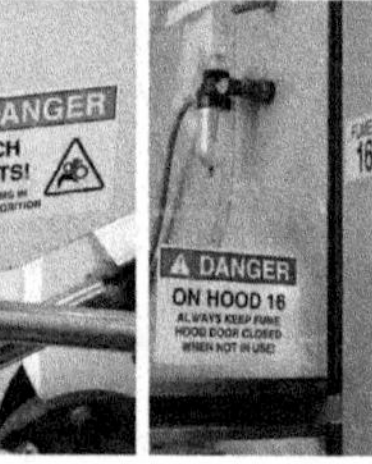

Labels that indicate danger

Walkways

Control Andons

Pressure Control

Oil-Level Control

Tension Control

LSSI
LEAN SIX SIGMA INSTITUTE

Office Andons

Document Trays

Files

Fire Extinguisher

Multi-skill Matrix Status

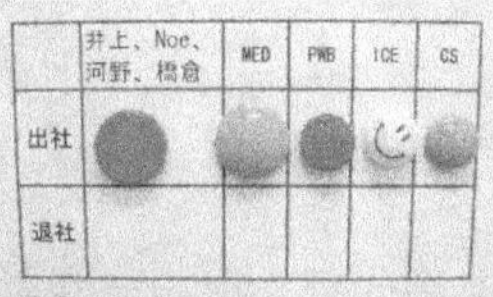

Personnel Assignments

Operations Andons

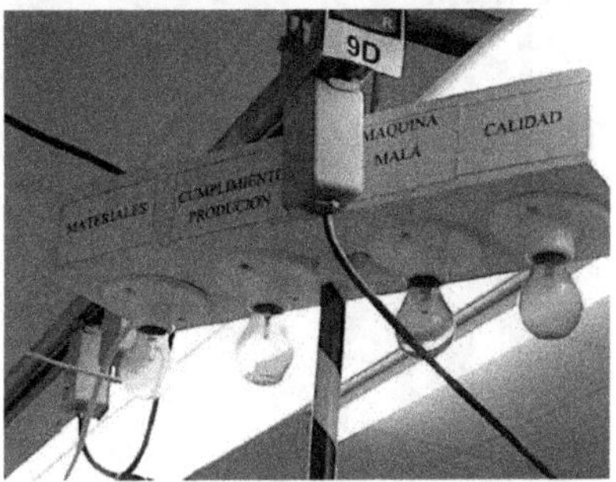

Examples of visual controls

Color-coded lubricant and liquid containers

Color-coded Bins

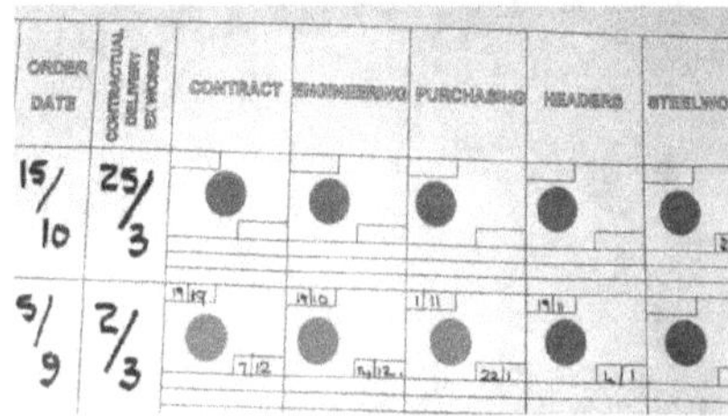

Fuguai Tagging Opportunity Cards

Color-coded Project Status sheets

Visual signal Andons

- The visual warning sensors inform the operator that there is a problem.

- These sensors use colors, alarms, and / or lights to get the workers' attention.

- They may be combined with a contact or energy sensor to get the workers' attention.

Healthcare Andons

- **Color-coded** Andons indicate the status of different patient areas.

- An Andon used in a **team meeting** to help guide actions.

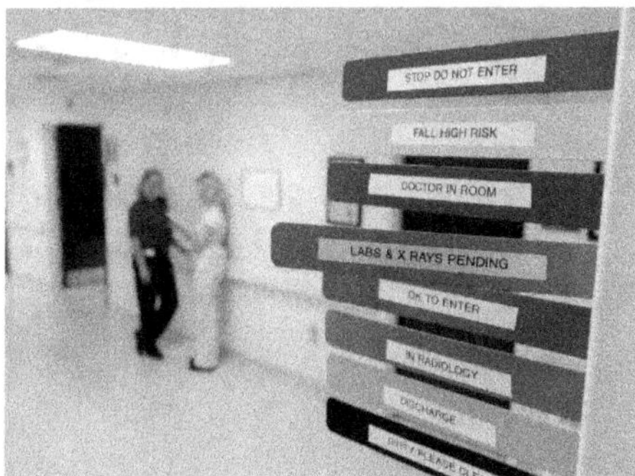

1. In your work area, identify opportunities to apply visual management and the corresponding Andon types.

2. Design a simple visual way to show what you have learned in this session.

3. Test the method you develop. Seek feedback from others who are involved in the system.

Standard Work Instructions

5

Learning objectives

1. Understand the essential elements of standardized work to ensure optimal performance.
2. Know the procedure for achieving standardization in any process.

Content

> Background
> What is Standard Work Instruction?
> Development of talent through standards
> Benefits

Background

Standard working methods were developed by Taiichi Ohno and Shigeo Shingo at Toyota during the 1950s and 1960s.

Shigeo Shingo

Taiichi Ohno

**«Where there is no standard, there can be no Kaizen.»
Taiichi Ohno**

What is a Standard?

A **standard** is a rule or example that provides clear explanations.

- Continuous improvement methods depend on identifying, setting, and improving standards.

- Standards form the baseline to analyze new opportunities for improvement.

The lack of standards creates confusion and frustration

Which is the right plug?

Which dial turns a specific burner?

Evolution of the "Stop" sign

- Today, the "Stop" sign is recognized all over the world

- However, in the early days, do you know what it was like?

There were no standards for road signs

Lack of standards was the problem

A lack of standards caused collisions,
injuries, and disorganization.

Types of standards

- Regulations

- Quality Standards

- Specifications

- Technical Standards

- Process Standards

- Manuals

- Notices

- Memos

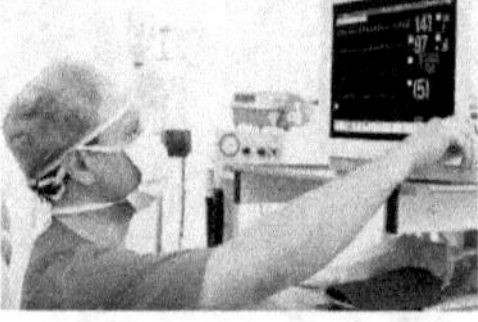

A good standard should be visual and help identify
abnormal situations in the processes.

LSSI
LEAN SIX SIGMA INSTITUTE

What is a Standard Work Instruction?

Standard Work Instructions (SWI) are instructions designed to ensure that processes are consistent, timely, and repeatable.

- They are printed and placed near the work station.

- The objectives and actual results of the use of the SWI are improvements in:

  - Increase in Quality of the finished product or servic

  - Consistency of the finished product or service

  - Increase in process performance

  - Employee safety

Work instructions

WORK INSTRUCTION

Area:		Operation:		
NO.	**SEQUENCE OF OPERATIONS**		**KEY POINTS**	
1	Pick up the material.		1.- Use both hands to pick up the material.	
2	Place the material on the work table.		1.- Use clamps to fix the piece in place.	
3	Place tips facing toward the edges.		1.- Make sure that the piece is properly balanced.	
4	Cut the piece to the desired length.		1.- Sharpen the cutting tool.	
5	Place cut pieces on the next table.		1.- Place them with the labeled side up.	
6				
7				

CHANGES						SAFETY CONSIDERATIONS
Date	Rev	ption of Change		Elim.	Approved	
						-Safety equipment must be used at all times.

It is recommended that operators, service providers, engineers, quality personnel, and HR staff all participate in the creation of work instructions to ensure all aspects are included.

LSSI
LEAN SIX SIGMA INSTITUTE

Type of Product or Service:	Prepared by:		Pg. 1 of 1

KEY POINTS REASONS	ILLUSTRATIONS

1.- Hold material firmly to avoid an incident.

1.- Prevents movement, which prevents defects and/or incidents.

1.- Facilitates cutting.

1.- Facilitates cutting.

1.- Facilitates identification.

SAFETY CONSIDERATIONS	SIGNATURES			
	Date	Shift	Supervisor	Operator

-Safety equipment must be used at all times.

Components of standard work

White Belt

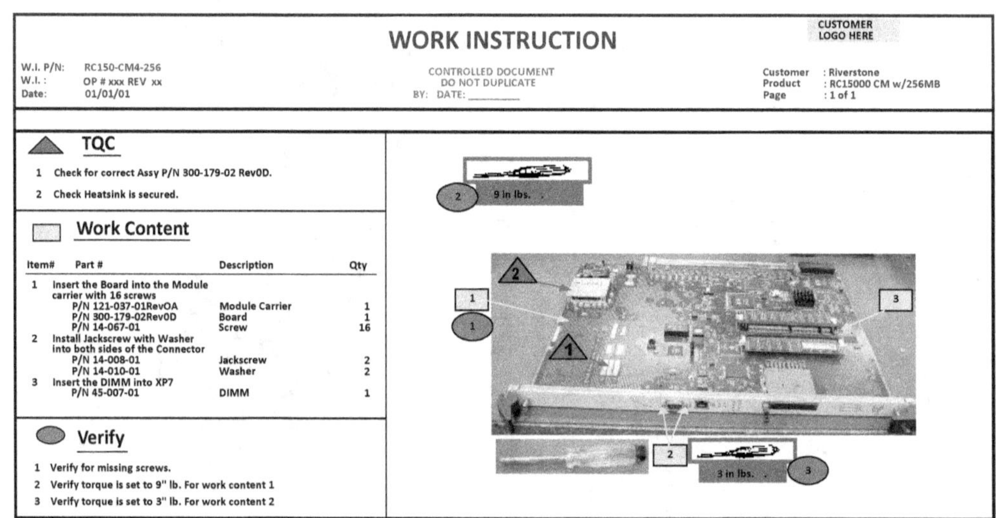

Job Instructions

Yellow Belt

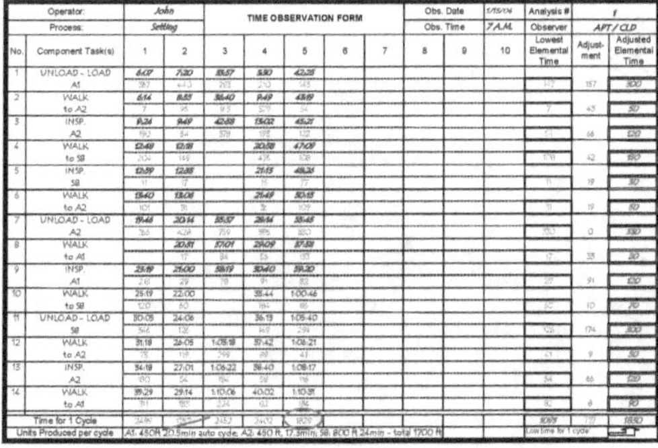

**Time Study Data
Collection Sheet**

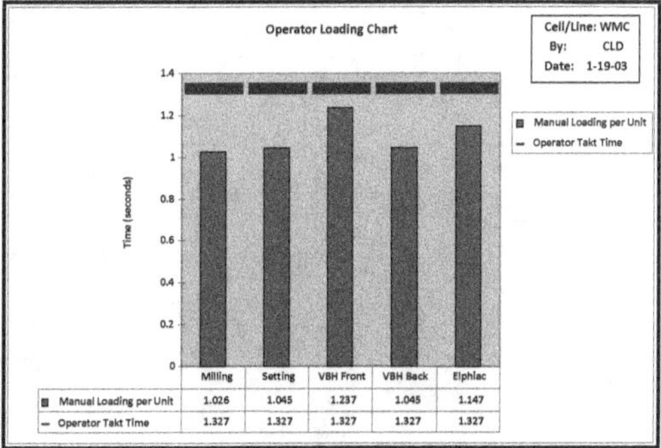

**Takt Time
Balance Chart**

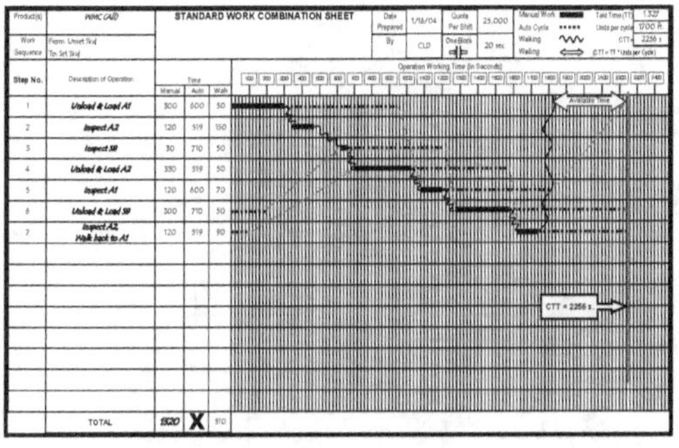

**Standard Work
Combination Sheet (SWCS)**

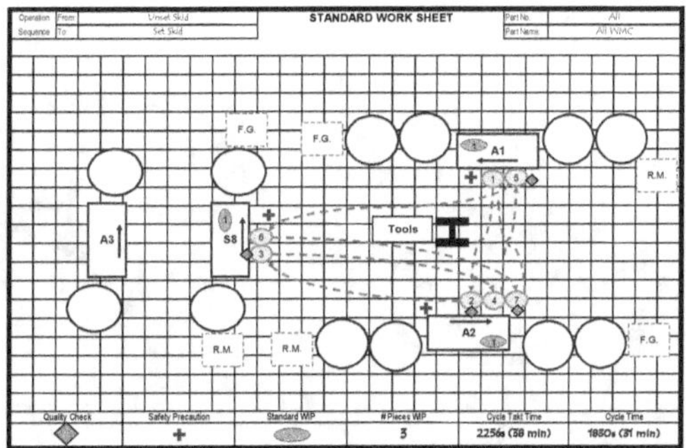

Standard Work Sheet (SWS)

Development of talent through TWI Standards

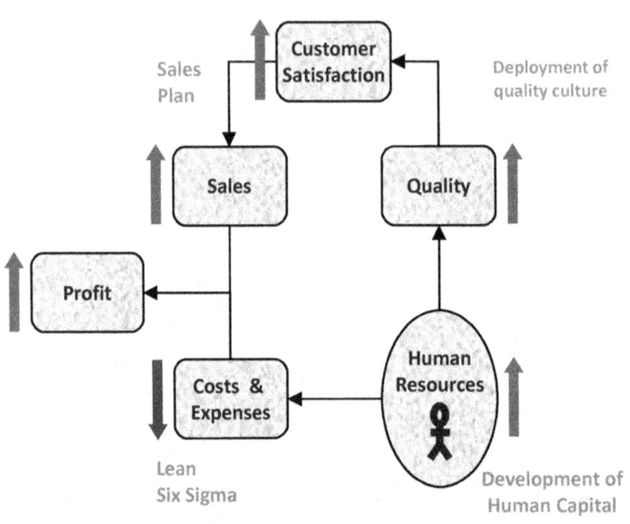

1. Prepare the Organization	2. Identify Critical Knowledge

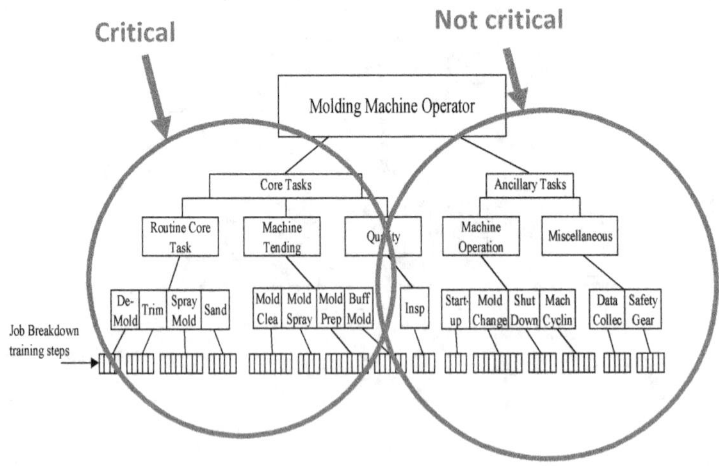

Job Instruction

Prepare the Worker

Present the Operation

Try Out Performance

Follow Up

3. Transfer Knowledge

4. Verify Learning

Name	Registet	Get. Info.	Diagnose
John Smith	1	3	4
Bob Hope	5	5	5
Robert Mills	3	4	2
Dave Jones	1	0	4

- Achieve process stability

  Standardization ensures that procedures are always performed identically to meet **safety**, **quality**, and **speed** standards.

- Provides a clear description of the activities in the workstation.

- Indicates the key points related to the operation.

- Establishes a baseline to evaluate and manage processes and assess their performance.

- Ensures safer and more effective operations.

- Establishes an invaluable information bank.

Note: SWIs are not neccesary for very simple or non-critical processes.

**Sales and operations planning.
S&OP in 14 steps**
Cristina Peña Andrés

**Lean Manufacturing.
Step by step**
Luis Socconini

**Lean Six Sigma.
Management System
for Leaders**
Luis Socconini, Carlo Reato

Substance Abuse Treatment
Ana Adan, Conrad Vilanou

**Practical guide to the
Incoterms 2020 rules**
David Soler

**Shipping & Commercial Case
Law**
Albert Badia

Lean Six Sigma Management. Certification Manual

Luis Socconini

Lean Six Sigma White Belt. Certification Manual

Luis Socconini

Lean Six Sigma Yellow Belt. Certification Manual

Luis Socconini

Lean Six Sigma Green Belt. Certification Manual

Luis Socconini

Lean Six Sigma Black Belt. Certification Manual

Luis Socconini

Lean Services. Certification Manual

Luis Socconini

MARGE BOOKS

València, 558 – 08026 Barcelona – Tel. +34-931 429 486 – marge@margebooks.com – www.margebooks.com